Dream Wide Awake

Your Self-Empowerment Guide
for Shifting from Balance to Synergy
and Daydreaming to Dream Doing

By Sherré DeMao, CSC, CGS

BASED ON THE TEACHINGS OF
THE NATIONALLY ACCLAIMED BOOK:

Me, Myself & Inc.

*A Synergized World,
An Energized Business,
Living Your Ultimate Life*

GreenCastle publishing

Published by GreenCastle Publishing
in association with GreenCastleIP

Illustration, Gary Palmer
Design, Layout & Production, SPARK Publications
Author Photo, Rae Images

Copyright ©2020 Sherré L. DeMao, CGS

All rights reserved. This workbook may not be reproduced in whole or in part without written permission from the author or publisher, except by reviewer who may quote brief passages in a review; nor may any part of this book be reproduced, stored in a retrievable system, or transmitted in any form or by any means, electronic, mechanical, photocopying, recording, or other without written permission from the publisher. For permissions call GreenCastleIP at 704.483.2941.

Library of Congress Cataloging-in-Publication Data
Library of Congress Control Number: 2019906025

January 2020, Softcover, ISBN: 978-0-9841051-4-4 / 0-9841051-4-X
January 2020, E-book, ISBN: 978-0-9841051-5-1 / 0-9841051-5-8

Printed in the U.S.A.

BODY, MIND & SPIRIT / Inspiration & Personal Growth
SELF-HELP / Personal Growth / Happiness
SELF-HELP / Personal Growth / Success

This workbook and audio series are dedicated
to my granddarlings, Emma Grace and Annabelle.

May you always dream wide awake
and forever feel the power from within
to honor who you are and were meant to be.

Praise for *Dream Wide Awake*

"This workbook will turn your life around. Whoever takes the actions set forth here WILL be transformed. The process is perfectly paced, leading the reader-participant to systematically build a foolproof foundation of self-knowledge using the author's brilliant MM&I framework. Extraordinary new possibilities open up for any of us willing to jump in, as we find ourselves freed from the tyrannical myth of 'Work/Life Balance' and empowered with the full synergy of values-goals alignment. Sherré DeMao uplifts, encourages, and inspires her readers at every turn. Transformation demands effort and courage, yet she makes it fun. I recommend that you embrace this workbook as your playbook for Life."

— Jane Ransom, author of *Self-Intelligence: The New Science-Based Approach for Reaching Your True Potential*

"Sherré takes us on a beautiful journey of understanding how life is about living synergistically every day … living a more purposeful life feeling inspired and empowered from the inside out."

— Sheila Unique, best-selling author of *Quick Shifts*

"Sherré L. DeMao is a master strategist, and in her workbook *Dream Wide Awake*, she shares a masterful framework, strategies, and exercises to help readers realize there is no such thing as balance and to look beyond that illusion to inside where all the answers are, such as who the real you is, your purpose, your passion, and your path. Highly recommended!"

— Whitney Vosburgh, author of the upcoming *Brand New Purpose: Turning grey into great* and coauthor of *Work The Future! Today*

"Sherré turned the concept of Work/Life Balance upside down and inside out when she introduced the idea of Synergy and honoring the three aspects of you in *Me, Myself & Inc.* Now, ten years later, she has brought an empowering process to knowing your WHY and how to embrace it and flourish through living it with total clarity and impassioned purpose. Her process in *Dream Wide Awake* is both common sense and brilliant in helping you unleash your inner wisdom and breathe renewed life into what you were meant to be doing."

— Gail Z. Martin, author of *Fresh Start Success: Reinvent Your Work, Reimagine Your Life, Reignite Your Passion*

"Sherré's *Dream Wide Awake* offers you the opportunity to take a self-guided retreat to awaken what's been dormant within and is screaming to get out! You'll discover and know three things without doubt: WHO you were meant to be, WHAT you were meant to be doing, and the underlying WHY that'll set your heart on fire. Her insights to the wishful and fearful thinking that can hold you back (I call it the GRAVITY of life) will help you defy gravity once and for all and take action to create your absolute best life. Dive into this work and Sherre's process. Emerge triumphant in all you'll do from that point forward."

– Matt Gersper, author of *Turning Inspiration into Action*, *The Belief Road Map*, and *Inspiring Women*

"I've never made more money nor been happier at my job. Anyone frustrated with their employment or business should read Sherré's book and go through her process of self-discovery. It will convince you to take the leap toward what you really want to be doing, just like it did for me."

– Rob Bignell, owner of Inventing Reality Editing Service and author of *7 Minutes a Day* series of books for authors

"Sherré DeMao brings us a dynamic new way of looking at work/life balance with her guided workbook *Dream Wide Awake*. She has created a compelling self-discovery process that will help uncover the life you are surely meant to live. A life-changing (and mind-shifting) way to gain clarity, conviction, and confidence!"

– Sharon Sayler, author of *What Your Body Says (and How to Master the Message)* and *Ditch Your Pitch – Speak from Your Heart and Instantly Intrigue Others*

"Brilliantly paradigm shifting! Like taking a deep breath, this book will have you look at how you integrate all the parts of your life into a joyful, fulfilling existence. You will discover your synergized purpose for the most wonderful journey you can take for the rest of your life. This is simply a 'must-read' workbook you won't want to put down."

–Teresa de Grosbois, #1 international best-selling author of *Mass Influence*

What is an MM&I MOMENT OF INSPIRATION?

Throughout this workbook, you will see special pages just like this randomly placed with the horizon faded in the background. These pages are to remind you to pause, take a deep breath, and along with that, take a Me, Myself & Inc. Moment of Inspiration to reflect or consider what the inspired quote is trying to tell you.

Want to be inspired on a weekly basis? Sign up for alerts to my weekly blog by going to www.sherredemao.com.

TABLE OF CONTENTS

Introduction 9

SECTION 1: From Balance To Synergy 11

    Chapter 1: Me, Myself & Inc. – The Three Aspects of YOU 13
    Chapter 2: Life Synergy 23
    Chapter 3: Your Goals, Your Values & YOU 55
    Chapter 4: Your Values = Living Your Life 59
    Chapter 5: Your Goals = Your Ultimate Life 69
    Chapter 6: Whose Goals Are They? 81
    Chapter 7: Aligning Values and Goals 89

SECTION 2: Three Promises – Rewiring Your Thinking 93

    Chapter 8: Find a Way or Make a Way 95
    Chapter 9: Don't Feel Guilty About Making Life Easier For Self 99
    Chapter 10: Being Open to All Possible Resources, Options & Support 103

SECTION 3: Wishful Thinking – From If Only to Absolutely! 107

    Chapter 11: If Only I Had More Confidence 109
    Chapter 12: If Only I Had More Choices, Fewer Choices 113
    Chapter 13: If Only I Had More Money 117
    Chapter 14: If Only I Had More Time 123
    Chapter 15: If Only I Had More Support 127

SECTION 4: Fearful Thinking – From Fear to Inspired Action 131

- Chapter 16: Fear of Success 133
- Chapter 17: Fear of Failure 137
- Chapter 18: Fear of Losing Control 141
- Chapter 19: Fear of Taking Risks 145
- Chapter 20: Fear of Being Ordinary 149
- Chapter 21: Fear of Letting Go 153

SECTION 5: Synergy in Motion 159

- Chapter 22: The Power of Purpose 161
- Chapter 23: The Power of HOPE 171
- Chapter 24: Short Term & Long Term Insights 175
- Chapter 25: Your Action Plan – The Power of CAN DO 179

About the Author 190

INTRODUCTION

When I wrote *Me, Myself & Inc.* a decade ago, I knew I was introducing a mind-shifting way of approaching entrepreneurship in the harsh reality that you cannot separate one's business from one's life. What was exciting to me was the fact that the concept of shifting from Work/Life Balance to Life Synergy was something that everyone was ready to embrace. My proclamation that Work/Life Balance doesn't work and never has was met with nodding heads and a sense of validation that resonated with whomever I talked to about this different way of approaching achievement, and more importantly, one's ultimately desired life.

As I continued to work with entrepreneurs and individuals, putting the teachings of the book into practice, I made some additional shifts of my own to make it even more powerful and effective. When the book was released, the Me, Myself & Inc. Quik Quiz assessment did not exist. The Synergy Quik Quiz has been tweaked for even more insight and value in combination with the MM&I Quik Quiz. The mind mapping process has also evolved to entirely shift away from the thinking that pits one's life against their work. It has been so rewarding to continue to evolve this concept into something tangible, effective, and doable.

I have lost count of the times I have had someone request that the book be available in audio and for a self-study course on embracing this shift to a synergy mindset. As I have led retreats entitled *Dream Wide Awake*, I realized that this is what this workbook and audio program should be called because through shifting to a synergy mindset, what may have seemed impossible will begin to look possible. It is what I like to call "dream doing" as opposed to daydreaming.

My goal in preparing this workbook and audio is to aid you in self-discovery and empowerment to truly live the life you have always wanted to live, with no limitations or restrictions, and with true clarity of purpose and passion.

By the time you complete this program and workbook, you will have a renewed outlook on what is possible for you and how you can go about achieving it. You will no longer feel as though external forces are working against you, but rather that your own internal forces are working within you.

You will be enlightened by the power of synergy ... the power of YOU!

> We as a society have had it all wrong. We have been focusing on the wrong side of the equation in this formula for a happier, more satisfying existence. It is not about balancing at all. It is something much more exciting and exhilarating!

SECTION 1

From Balance to Synergy

Work/Life Balance has become the mantra of executive coaches, training professionals, spiritual advisors, magazine articles, and corporate values statements for decades. Look up the word "balance" in the dictionary, and the definition ranges from "a state of equilibrium or parity characterized by the cancellation of one set of forces by equal opposing forces" to "a satisfying arrangement or proportion of parts or elements." And herein lies the problem. We are viewing our personal and work lives as elements, parts, and opposing forces. Everything is separate and in conflict, pulling and tugging at us from all directions.

The fact that Work/Life Balance pits work against life is a perfect example. Isn't work a part of our lives? So why is it separated out as something working against our ability to live the way we want to live?

This section will help you shift away from believing that Work/Life Balance is the answer, when it is actually the problem. You will be enlightened to a more empowering way of approaching your everyday existence. You will be enlightened to synergy.

> "The most profound aspect of all of this is that balance has us looking outside of ourselves and allowing everything outside of us to influence and dictate how we should be, when the reality is we should be guided and empowered from within by who we are and want to be."

CHAPTER 1
Me, Myself & Inc. – The Three Aspects of YOU

Look up the word "synergy" in the dictionary, and you will find definitions such as "the interaction of two or more forces so that their combined effect is greater than the sum of the individual effects" or "cooperative interaction that creates an enhanced combined effect." No conflict, no forces going against one another, but rather a true sense of harmony being achieved in the most desirable way. While a balance mindset rips you apart, a synergy mindset makes you whole.

The beauty of shifting to Life Synergy as a way of being is it starts with YOU! It looks inside at who you are and how you are through exploring the three aspects that we all possess:

ME = The family, friends, and community YOU

MYSELF = The individual YOU

INC. = The business owner, professional, or at-work YOU

The ME aspect of YOU

This facet of you focuses on the aspect that is shared with everyone else. It is the relationship part of you that interacts with others. None of us are solo in this world. We cannot live without interacting with others. Human beings were meant to relate on a level that no other species relates emotionally, intellectually, physically, and spiritually. The more we feel connected with others, the more we feel connected to ourselves. Take a moment to consider all the people you interact with on a daily basis, and don't limit it to whom you consider yourself close to in family and friends or at work.

As an exercise, list all the people you have interacted with in the past week, from people who have served you to those who have entertained you, not just face-to-face, but in any way at all. Note next to these people what you enjoyed or did not enjoy.

_____
_____
_____
_____
_____
_____
_____

The MYSELF aspect of YOU

This facet of you focuses on the aspect of you that is solely you and is what makes you tick. It is also the part of you that intuitively knows what is best when you fully embrace who you are and were meant to be. The problem is that we have allowed the balance mindset to impact who we think we are or should be based on external influences instead of internal knowing. Society and our interactions with others carry great weight in how we define ourselves and how we think we must be. In many ways, we don't take the time we need to understand who we truly are as individuals. This is sad and all too often true. We identify with others to the extent that we believe we are like them instead of who we actually are as a person.

As an exercise, write words that you believe describe you. Don't sensor or think too much about it. Just write words. We will visit these words later.

_____
_____
_____
_____
_____

The INC. aspect of YOU

This facet of you focuses on the aspect of you that works to earn a living or make living all that it can be. However, I want to make something clear here. If you are not working in a job right now as is defined by society, you still have an INC. aspect of you. This aspect of you takes all of the qualities that make you unique and enables you to be a contributor to society in small and profound ways. We all have a contribution to make in this world, and we each were put on this Earth to fully embrace and realize our ultimate purpose.

How do you believe you currently contribute to society? List whatever comes to mind.

How would you like to be contributing to society either through your profession or philanthropy that you are not currently engaged in?

MM&I Quik Quiz

To begin the process of shifting to synergy, you must first understand how well you are honoring the three aspects of you. The reason you may be frustrated or not fully satisfied in your life is because you are not fully embracing the three aspects of you and all that you can be. Take this Quik Quiz to gain insight, inspiration, and the ability to identify ways you can bring those missing aspects of you into being.

Check the statements below that apply to you, then reference the key on the next page.

- ☐ 1. I enjoy regular and meaningful interaction with family members.
- ☐ 2. I enjoy regular and meaningful interaction with friends.
- ☐ 3. I enjoy meaningful and intimate interaction with a spouse or significant other.
- ☐ 4. I enjoy and explore my community with my friends, family, spouse, or significant other.
- ☐ 5. I make it a priority to allocate time for myself on a regular basis, so I can recharge, refocus, and relax.
- ☐ 6. I have hobbies or things I like to do just for me and my own self-expression, self-development, and fulfillment.
- ☐ 7. I believe that taking care of me is a priority, and I therefore regularly exercise and eat right to nourish my mind, spirit, and being.
- ☐ 8. I enjoy and regularly learn new things and explore new ideas or places alone and with others as a way of continually bringing more to my life and my work.
- ☐ 9. I look forward to making a difference each day and cannot wait to see what the day brings in both challenges and opportunities.
- ☐ 10. I believe that I am doing exactly what I was meant to do as a profession or way of making a difference and get great satisfaction from my efforts and contributions.
- ☐ 11. I gain great satisfaction and inspiration from the people I engage with and do business with who reinforce that the work I do makes a difference.
- ☐ 12. I have developed friendships through my work that are meaningful and valued, but also have a network of friends outside of my work that is stimulating and important in my life.

ME – The friends, family, and community YOU

If you checked 1, 2, 3, and 4 . . . . . you have embraced and are enjoying this aspect of you. If any one of these were not checked, this is where you are not being fulfilled and could be part of your frustration. Take a look at what you did check to see how you can potentially create opportunities for bringing the ones not checked into reality. If you did not check any in this area, it is time to reconnect with this aspect of you by reaching out to family, friends, and your community to stimulate regular and meaningful interaction and participation in your life.

Take a moment to write what you most miss or feel could be better in this aspect of you based on what you checked and did not check.

_____
_____
_____
_____
_____
_____
_____
_____

Review what you have checked, and elaborate on what you value most about these varied interactions and relationships.

_____
_____
_____
_____
_____
_____
_____
_____

MYSELF — The individual YOU

If you checked 5, 6, 7, and 8 . . . . . you have embraced and are enjoying this aspect of you. If any one of these were not checked, then you are allowing everything else in your work and your life to be more important than taking care of you. The irony is that by taking care of and nurturing you, you are in a better place and space to enjoy others, contribute, and interact in more meaningful ways with others and in your work. So whatever you did not check, make it your priority to bring the individual, authentic you back into your life.

Take a moment to write what you can do to better honor this aspect of you based on what you did not check off. What could improve? What is stopping you?

_____

_____

_____

_____

_____

_____

Review what you have checked and elaborate on what is so gratifying. What are you doing well? What is encouraging to you?

_____

_____

_____

_____

_____

_____

INC. – The business, professional, or contributing YOU

If you checked 9, 10, 11, and 12 . . . . . you have embraced and are enjoying this aspect of you. If any one of these were not checked, then you are allowing yourself to be in a place or space that is not gratifying or fulfilling you in the work that you do or the contribution you could be making to society. Take a look at what you did not check and consider why.

Take a moment to write what you feel is missing based on what you did not check. Then make a list of things you can do, small things, that can shift you to more fulfilling and meaningful work.

_____
_____
_____
_____
_____
_____
_____

Review what you have checked and elaborate on what is so rewarding.

_____
_____
_____
_____
_____
_____
_____

Q&A Self Assessment Action List

Based on your review and notes from the MM&I Quik Quiz, list at least 10 things you would like to start doing or an action step you will take to better honor the three aspects of you.

1.
2.
3.
4.
5.
6.
7.
8.
9.
10.

MM&I MOMENT OF INSPIRATION

*"It's called being in the moment …
and intuition rewards this
mentality in glorious ways."*

- Sherré DeMao -

"Synergy doesn't force you to wait for or give up what you really want. It doesn't make you feel like what you want is in conflict with something else that you want. Synergy is energy. It gives you a sense of empowerment versus depleting your power."

CHAPTER 2
Life Synergy

The beauty of synergy is it focuses on building upon what is already in place. What makes it so empowering is it first focuses on you and the three aspects of you. Synergy is an inside-out process, which puts you in the driver's seat.

As I stated in Chapter 1, the concept of Work/Life Balance has done us a disservice because it has us looking at everything externally around us and then making decisions based on what is not in our control versus what is in our control. Before you can begin to make the full shift to a synergy mindset, you must understand how mired you are in the balance mindset.

Synergy Quik Quiz

Complete to better understand where you are right now in your attempts to balance, so you can shift away from your balance mindset and take true action through a more gratifying synergy mindset.

Check the statements below that apply to you, then reference the key that follows.

- ❑ **1.** I have specific personal goals unrelated to work or business.

- ❑ **2.** I have determined action steps to achieve my personal goals.

- ❑ **3.** I have specific business/career goals, both long term and short term.

- ❑ **4.** I have a strategy for helping me achieve these business/career goals.

- ❑ **5.** I am more successful at reaching my business/career goals.

OR (Choose either 5 or 6 or none if neither apply)

- ❑ **6.** I am more successful at reaching my personal goals.

❏   **7.** Because of my personal goals, I accept that I cannot fully realize my business/career goals at this time.

OR (Choose either 7 or 8 or none if neither apply)

❏   **8.** Because of my business/career goals, I accept that I cannot fully realize my personal goals at this time.

Check ONLY ONE statement below that describes your current view. If none apply, check none of them.

❏   **9.** I am achieving neither my business/career nor personal goals to my satisfaction.

❏   **10.** I am content, but there are still aspects of my life and work that I know could be even better.

❏   **11.** I don't have any specific personal goals. I'm totally focused on my business/career at this time.

❏   **12.** I reach my personal and business/career goals, but it still isn't enough.

NOTE: Did you only check one answer (or none) in this final section?

Synergy Quik Quiz Answer Reference Key

(write numbers checked from previous pages above)

    Find the section that most closely matches the answers you selected, then answer the questions that follow for added self-exploration and understanding.

    If you checked 1, 2, 6, and 7 . . . . . you are entirely personally driven and focused. You don't have any work or career goals, perhaps because working is not something that is necessary or important to you in your life or because you are retired or temporarily unemployed and between opportunities. The reasons for having no career goals and strategies can be many. However, the INC. aspect of you is not just a paid-to-work aspect. It is about you making a contribution beyond yourself. If you believe choosing personal endeavors only must be your choice in order to have balance in your life, then you may be limiting yourself without realizing it. While you accept that you are fully aware of this choice, at the same time, since you are better at achieving your personal goals, there may be an underlying reason that needs to be honestly explored and understood.

Where are you finding satisfaction or contentment?

_____

_____

_____

_____

_____

Where are you finding the least contentment?

_____

_____

_____

_____

_____

If you could do anything at all and knew you could not fail, what would you love to accomplish?

_____
_____
_____
_____
_____

Go back and review your answers to the MM&I Quik Quiz. What insights can you note here based on your answers in what you checked and did not check?

_____
_____
_____
_____
_____

If you checked 1, 2, 3, 4, and 9 . . . . . you are driven, but stuck.

You are determined and have much you want to accomplish, yet it seems you just aren't achieving what you are striving to achieve. You likely feel pulled in a million directions and feel as though there is so much out of your control that is impacting your ability to get what you are trying to get accomplished. A balance mindset is the reason why you feel as though the outside continues to crash in on your dreams. Even though you are focused on actions and steps to get you where you want to go, you feel limited or prohibited in ways that you may not fully comprehend or understand.

Which areas of your life have your head spinning and make you feel overwhelmed?

_____
_____
_____
_____

Which areas of your career have your head spinning and make you feel overwhelmed?

Where are you finding the greatest satisfaction?

Where are you finding the least satisfaction?

Go back and review your answers to the MM&I Quik Quiz. What insights can you note here based on your answers in what you checked and did not check?

If you checked 1, 2, 3, 4, 5, and 8 . . . . . you are focused on work and achieving at work. While you have personal goals and have identified steps to achieve them, you have fallen victim to the balance mindset because you believe that your focus must be entirely on your work and career. While you accept that you are fully aware of this choice, at the same time, since you are better at achieving your career goals versus your personal goals, there may be an underlying reason you are choosing not to put any of your attention into your personal endeavors, which needs to be honestly explored and understood.

Where are you finding satisfaction or contentment?

_____
_____
_____
_____
_____

Where are you finding the least contentment?

_____
_____
_____
_____
_____

If you could do anything at all and knew you could not fail, what would you love to accomplish?

_____
_____
_____
_____
_____

Go back and review your answers to the MM&I Quik Quiz. What insights can you note here based on your answers in what you checked and did not check?

_____
_____
_____
_____
_____

If you checked 1, 2, 3, 4, 6, and 7 . . . . . you are obsessed and preoccupied with personal endeavors. While you have career/professional goals and have identified strategies to achieve them, you have fallen victim to the balance mindset because you believe that your focus must be entirely on personal endeavors. While you accept that you are fully aware of this choice, at the same time, since you are better at achieving your personal goals versus your career goals, there may be an underlying reason you are choosing not to put any of your attention into your career, which needs to be honestly explored and understood. You may feel ungratified in the work you do or perhaps don't consider your job as a true career, so your heart is not as into it. Perhaps the goals and strategies at work are dictated versus something you have determined and embraced.

Where are you finding satisfaction or contentment?

_____
_____
_____
_____

Where are you finding the least contentment?

_____
_____
_____
_____

Life Synergy

If you could do anything at all and knew you could not fail, what would you love to accomplish?

_____
_____
_____
_____
_____

Go back and review your answers to the MM&I Quik Quiz. What insights can you note here based on your answers in what you checked and did not check?

_____
_____
_____
_____
_____

If you checked 1, 2, 3, 4, and 10 . . . . . you are content yet want even more. You are content with what you have accomplished thus far, yet you also believe your life could be even better. You enjoy striving and thriving and believe there is always something more that can be done, and you want to explore those possibilities and see where they may lead you.

Where are you finding the greatest contentment?

_____
_____
_____
_____
_____

Where are you finding the least contentment?

If you could do anything at all and knew you could not fail, what would you love to accomplish?

Go back and review your answers to the MM&I Quik Quiz. What insights can you note here based on your answers in what you checked and did not check?

If you checked 1, 2, 3, 4, and 12 . . . . . you are accomplished yet unsatisfied. You have achieved a great deal, yet you still want more. It may be that you have played it a little too safe because of a balance mindset. There may be goals that just seem so "out there" and so "bodacious" that you have convinced yourself they are beyond reach. It is also possible you may be ready for something totally different to challenge you.

Where are you finding your greatest satisfaction?

_____
_____
_____
_____
_____

Where are you finding the least satisfaction?

_____
_____
_____
_____
_____

If you could do anything at all and knew you could not fail, what would you love to accomplish?

_____
_____
_____
_____
_____

Go back and review your answers to the MM&I Quik Quiz. What insights can you note here based on your answers in what you checked and did not check?

_____
_____
_____
_____

If you checked 1, 2, 6, and 10 . . . . . you are more personally focused. You feel more successful in your personal life, most likely because it is more gratifying and brings you the greatest satisfaction. The fact that you have specific personal goals and action plans yet do not have specific business/career goals and a strategy indicates one of two things. The first option is that you don't have to work; therefore, your personal life is all you are focused upon. It seems easier and more fluid, so you can focus on it more easily. The second option is that your personal life has posed many demands upon you, and you have accepted the fact that it is necessary to place less emphasis on your business/career success. If you think you have no choice but to choose one over the other right now, then you are in a balancing mindset versus a synergy mindset. You are pitting one against the other subconsciously, while not intentionally.

Where are you finding your greatest satisfaction?

Where are you finding the least satisfaction?

Is having work that you love doing important to you, whether paid or unpaid? And if so, what is it you enjoy doing?

If personal demands are the main reason for being so personally focused, how does this make you feel about your life overall? Be honest.

_____
_____
_____
_____
_____

Go back and review your answers to the MM&I Quik Quiz. What insights can you note here based on your answers in what you checked and did not check?

_____
_____
_____
_____
_____

If you checked 1, 2, 3, 7, and 10 . . . . . you are sacrificing career goals for personal demands. You feel you must sacrifice your business or career aspirations due to your personal goals or situation. Even if your personal life has posed many demands upon you, it doesn't mean you cannot have business/career success too. If you think you have no choice but to choose one over the other right now, then you are in a balancing mindset versus a synergy mindset. You are pitting one against the other. By putting your career goals on the back burner, so to speak, you are most likely missing and not seeing opportunities to synergize because you are too personally focused. You are subconsciously checked out on the career side of things even though you are professionally engaged in what you do for a living on a day-to-day basis.

Where are you finding your greatest satisfaction?

_____
_____
_____
_____

Where are you finding the least satisfaction?

_____
_____
_____
_____
_____

Is having work that you love doing important to you? And if so, what is it you enjoy doing about the work that you do? What is missing from the work that you are currently doing?

_____
_____
_____
_____
_____

If personal demands are the main reason for being so personally focused, how does this make you feel about your life overall? Be honest.

_____
_____
_____
_____
_____

Go back and review your answers to the MM&I Quik Quiz. What insights can you note here based on your answers in what you checked and did not check?

_____
_____
_____
_____

If you checked 1, 2, 7, and 9 . . . . . you are focused upon personal demands, and frustrated. You feel you must focus all of your energy right now upon your personal situation and desires. Even if your personal life has posed many demands upon you, it doesn't mean you cannot have career satisfaction too. The problem is that you are not realizing personal satisfaction, in spite of putting all your focus upon it, so adding career to the mix would only overwhelm you even more. If you think you have no choice but to choose one over the other right now, then you are in a balancing mindset versus a synergy mindset. Your frustration may be limiting your ability to see opportunities personally and professionally. You feel great pressure in accomplishing what you are trying to accomplish in your personal life, and it is weighing heavily on you.

Where are you finding any satisfaction, no matter how small and inconsequential it may seem right now?

Where are you finding the least satisfaction?

Is having work that you love doing important to you? And if so, what is it you enjoy doing about the work that you do? What is missing from the work that you are currently doing?

If personal demands are the main reason for being so personally focused, how does this make you feel about your life overall? Be honest.

_____
_____
_____
_____
_____

Go back and review your answers to the MM&I Quik Quiz. What insights can you note here based on your answers in what you checked and did not check?

_____
_____
_____
_____
_____
_____

If you checked 1, 2, 7, and 10 . . . . . you are focused upon personal demands. You feel you must focus all of your energy right now upon your personal situation and desires. Even if your personal life has posed many demands upon you, it doesn't mean you cannot have career satisfaction too. If you think you have no choice but to choose one over the other right now, then you are in a balancing mindset versus a synergy mindset. You may not know fully what you want to do or were meant to do as a career, so as a result it is difficult to focus upon it or set goals around it. You are subconsciously checked out on the career side of things and gain your contentment from what is getting accomplished personally.

Where are you finding your greatest contentment?

_____
_____
_____
_____
_____

Life Synergy

Where are you finding the least contentment?

_____
_____
_____
_____

Is having work that you love doing important to you? What is it you enjoy doing about the work that you do or have done? What is missing from the work that you are currently doing?

_____
_____
_____
_____

If personal demands are the main reason for being so personally focused, how does this make you feel about your life overall? Be honest.

_____
_____
_____
_____

Go back and review your answers to the MM&I Quik Quiz. What insights can you note here based on your answers in what you checked and did not check?

_____
_____
_____
_____

If you checked 1, 3, 4, 5, and 10 . . . . . you are more business/career focused. Your personal goals are just wishes and dreams and not tangible based on how you approach achieving them. While you have personal goals, that is as far as you have taken them, with no focused action in place to make them a reality. On the other hand, you approach your business/career goals with a strategy to help achieve them and, as a result, are more successful at achieving them. This may be because you gain greater satisfaction from your work over your personal life and, therefore, place more of your focus on your career.

Where are you finding your greatest satisfaction?

_____
_____
_____
_____
_____

Where are you finding the least satisfaction?

_____
_____
_____
_____
_____

Why do you feel you cannot focus upon your personal goals at this time?

_____
_____
_____
_____
_____

Is having work that you love doing important to you? And if so, what is it you enjoy doing about the work that you do? What is missing from the work that you are currently doing?

_____
_____
_____
_____
_____

If career demands are the main reason for being so career focused, how does this make you feel about your life overall? Be honest.

_____
_____
_____
_____
_____

Go back and review your answers to the MM&I Quik Quiz. What insights can you note here based on your answers in what you checked and did not check?

_____
_____
_____
_____
_____

If you checked 1, 3, 6, and 9 . . . . . you are dream wishing versus dream doing. Your goals are just wishes and not tangible based on how you approach achieving them. While you have goals, that is as far as you have taken them, with no focused action or strategies in place to make them a reality. You are likely in a constant tug of war between both personal and business/career or making a meaningful difference, and so nothing is getting accomplished in your eyes. You do a little here and a little there, but are not seeing any real progress.

Where are you finding your greatest satisfaction?

Where are you finding the least satisfaction?

What is your greatest source of frustration, the reason you feel you cannot reach any of your goals? List all that come to mind.

Is having work that you love doing important to you? And if so, what is it you enjoy doing about the work that you do? What is missing from the work that you are currently doing?

Go back and review your answers to the MM&I Quik Quiz. What insights can you note here based on your answers in what you checked and did not check?

_____
_____
_____
_____
_____

If you checked 1, 3, 8, and 10 . . . . . you are dream wishing and sacrificing. Your goals are just wishes and not tangible based on how you approach achieving them. While you have goals, that is as far as you have taken them, with no focused action or strategies in place to make them a reality. You are feeling pressure to achieve on the business/career side of things, causing you to feel you must sacrifice personal goals in order to achieve what you desire to achieve on the work front. If you think you have no choice but to choose one over the other right now, then you are in a balancing mindset versus a synergy mindset. You are pitting one against the other.

Where are you finding your greatest contentment?

_____
_____
_____
_____
_____

Where are you finding the least contentment?

_____
_____
_____
_____
_____

Why do you feel you cannot focus upon your personal goals at this time? What is your reasoning for sacrificing some of what you want to accomplish?

_____
_____
_____
_____
_____

Is having work that you love doing important to you? And if so, what is it you enjoy doing about the work that you do? What is missing from the work that you are currently doing?

_____
_____
_____
_____
_____

If career demands are the main reason for being so career focused, how does this make you feel about your life overall? Be honest.

_____
_____
_____
_____
_____

Go back and review your answers to the MM&I Quik Quiz. What insights can you note here based on your answers in what you checked and did not check?

_____
_____
_____
_____
_____

If you checked 3, 4, 5, and 10 . . . . . you are more business/career focused. You are more focused upon your work and career and perhaps believe this is how it needs to be right now. While you may have personal desires and wants, you don't feel the need to focus upon them or express them at this time. You gain more gratification from your work. You approach your business/career goals with a strategy to help achieve them and, as a result, are more successful at achieving them, which adds to your contentment. This may be because you gain greater satisfaction from your work over your personal life and, therefore, place more of your focus on your career. You are not trying to balance at all yet do feel that there is more to life than what you currently are experiencing and that it could be even better.

Where are you finding your greatest contentment?

_____
_____
_____
_____
_____

Where are you finding the least contentment?

_____
_____
_____
_____
_____

Why do you feel you cannot focus upon your personal life at this time?

_____
_____
_____
_____

Is having work that you love doing important to you? And if so, what is it you enjoy doing about the work that you do? What is missing from the work that you are currently doing?

_____
_____
_____
_____

If career demands are the main reason for being so career focused, how does this make you feel about your life overall? Be honest.

_____
_____
_____
_____

Go back and review your answers to the MM&I Quik Quiz. What insights can you note here based on your answers in what you checked and did not check?

_____
_____
_____
_____

If you checked 3, 4, 5, and 11 . . . . . you are totally business/career focused. You are totally focused upon your work and career and perhaps believe this is how it needs to be right now. While you may have personal desires and wants, you don't feel the need to focus upon them or express them at this time. You believe your work defines who you are to a certain extent. You approach your business/career goals with a strategy to help achieve them and, as a result, are more successful at achieving them. You gain greater satisfaction from your work over your personal life and, therefore, intentionally place more of your focus on your career. You are not trying to balance at all yet likely do feel that there is more to life than what you currently are experiencing, which only makes you drive yourself harder on the career front.

Where are you finding your greatest satisfaction?

_____
_____
_____
_____
_____

Where are you finding the least satisfaction?

_____
_____
_____
_____
_____

Why do you feel you cannot focus upon your personal life at this time?

_____
_____
_____
_____
_____

Is having work that you love doing important to you? And if so, what is it you enjoy doing about the work that you do? What is missing from the work that you are currently doing?

_____
_____
_____
_____
_____

If career demands are the main reason for being so career focused, how does this make you feel about your life overall? Be honest.

_____
_____
_____
_____
_____

Go back and review your answers to the MM&I Quik Quiz. What insights can you note here based on your answers in what you checked and did not check?

_____
_____
_____
_____
_____

If you checked 3, 4, 5, 8, and 11 . . . . . you are a workaholic, business/career driven and like it that way. You are totally focused upon your work and career and perhaps believe this is how it needs to be right now. You don't feel the need to focus upon personal desires or goals at this time. Perhaps you believe you can focus more on them once you achieve the level you have deemed acceptable or successful for you. You believe your work defines who you are to a certain extent, and you are quite good and accomplished in your work. You approach your business/career goals with a strategy to help achieve them and, as a result, are more successful at achieving them. You gain greater satisfaction from your work over your personal life and, therefore, intentionally place all of your focus on your career. You are not trying to balance at all yet likely do feel that there is more to life than what you currently are experiencing, which only makes you drive yourself harder on the career front.

Where are you finding your greatest satisfaction?

___

Where are you finding the least satisfaction?

___

Why do you feel you cannot focus upon your personal life at this time?

___

Is having work that you love doing important to you? And if so, what is it you enjoy doing about the work that you do? What is missing from the work that you are currently doing?

_____
_____
_____
_____
_____

If career demands are the main reason for being so career focused, how does this make you feel about your life overall? Be honest.

_____
_____
_____
_____
_____

Go back and review your answers to the MM&I Quik Quiz. What insights can you note here based on your answers in what you checked and did not check?

_____
_____
_____
_____
_____

If you checked 3, 4, and 11 . . . . . you are feeling internal pressure to focus entirely on career pursuits. You are totally focused upon your work and career and perhaps believe this is how it needs to be right now. You don't feel the need to focus upon personal desires or goals at this time. Perhaps you believe you can focus more on them once you achieve the level you have deemed acceptable or successful for you. You approach your business/career goals with a strategy to help achieve them, but have not yet attained the level of success you desire. You may feel you need more time to put everything you've got to give into your career right now. You may gain greater satisfaction from your work over your personal life and, therefore, intentionally place more of your focus on your career. You are not trying to balance at all yet likely do feel that there is more to life than what you currently are experiencing, which only makes you drive yourself harder on the career front.

Where are you finding your greatest satisfaction in your life?

___

Where are you finding the least satisfaction in your life?

___

Why do you feel you cannot focus upon your personal life at this time?

___

Is having work that you love doing important to you? And if so, what is it you enjoy doing about the work that you do? What is missing from the work that you are currently doing?

_____
_____
_____
_____
_____

If career demands are the main reason for being so career focused, how does this make you feel about your life overall? Be honest.

_____
_____
_____
_____
_____

Go back and review your answers to the MM&I Quik Quiz. What insights can you note here based on your answers in what you checked and did not check?

_____
_____
_____
_____
_____

If you checked 6 and 10 . . . . . you are fluttering through life. With no personal or business/career goals and no strategy or action steps to achieve them, you are literally allowing life to happen to you versus embracing what your life can truly be. You feel more successful in your personal life, most likely because it is more gratifying and brings you the greatest satisfaction. You don't feel that you have to think about it as much, and it seems to flow in a way that makes you feel content. You feel fortunate in many ways, but there are things you still want to accomplish and still want to do. Who you are or the things that you are most passionate about have not been fully realized and explored.

Where are you finding your greatest contentment?

_____
_____
_____
_____
_____

Where are you finding the least contentment?

_____
_____
_____
_____
_____

Why do you feel you are more successful at reaching your personal goals, and why don't you have any specific personal goals right now?

_____
_____
_____
_____
_____

Is having work that you love doing important to you? And if so, what is it you enjoy doing that would like to be doing more? What is missing that you would like to be doing?

_____
_____
_____
_____
_____

Go back and review your answers to the MM&I Quik Quiz. What insights can you note here based on your answers in what you checked and did not check?

_____
_____
_____
_____
_____

Q&A Self-Exploration

Take a moment to review all of your answers in the section that applied to you. What additional thoughts and insights are coming to mind as you review your answers as a whole?

_____
_____
_____
_____
_____
_____
_____

"The problem with the balance mindset is it forces you to focus on what is out of balance. When you are continuously reacting versus being proactive in your attempts to achieve, you are never able to get ahead, or at least that is how it feels."

CHAPTER 3
Your Goals, Your Values & YOU

I equate the balance mindset to the vaudeville performer who is frantically keeping spinning plates balancing on the thin wires shooting up from the floor. It is impressive at first to see all those plates spinning from the outside looking in. However, for the person spinning the plates, it is exhausting, rushing here and there to keep each plate spinning as one starts to wobble. Eventually, a plate comes crashing down because there just wasn't the ability to deal with what was causing it to wobble at the time.

Everything outside of you is impacting what is happening inside of you. How can that be gratifying or encouraging at all? My real "aha," as I stated earlier, is when I realized that we need to stop focusing on what is happening on the outside as our compass for existence and focus instead on what is inside of us.

Do you have goals that you revisit every year at the beginning of each New Year, and while they remain a goal, they are basically rolling over to the next year because you haven't been able to focus upon them or achieve them to your satisfaction? Write these goals here.

_____

_____

_____

_____

Are some of your goals actually related to what is causing you great frustration or anxiety in your life? Write these goals here.

_____

_____

_____

_____

Are some of your goals focused on fixing something, correcting something, or changing something about yourself, a situation, or others? Write these goals here.

_____
_____
_____
_____
_____

In the chapters to follow, I am going to help you approach setting goals in a different way. You will gain a better understanding of what makes you unlike anyone else in how you think, how you like to interact with others, and what is important to you and for you. You may also find that the goals you have written above are no longer goals you desire to embrace.

MM&I MOMENT OF INSPIRATION

"Opportunities abound. Simply think beyond what you see, and vision beyond what you think."

- Sherré DeMao -

> Understanding your values and what is at the core of who you are is critical to achieving more, feeling satisfied, and being content with your life as a whole. Too many people have never taken the time to really get to know and embrace themselves and then wonder why they feel lost or misunderstood.

CHAPTER 4
Your Values = Living Your Life

If you don't understand what is truly meaningful and important to you at the core of who you are, how can you possibly know which goals will give you the greatest satisfaction in your life? Your values will help you better understand what you love, what you don't enjoy, what you believe is important, and so much more.

When I first started working with others in helping them achieve their goals through embracing the three aspects of themselves, I started with them sharing their goals. Then it became clear that understanding one's values was critical to everything in the process. So I started focusing on understanding core values first, and then moved to goals.

One important distinction needs to be made. Beliefs that you have are not values, though they could be. I know this sounds confusing; however, it is important to understand. Your true core values are at the very heart and soul of who you are as a person. Beliefs can be imposed upon you to the point that you actually think they are a value; the reality is that you have been made to believe them through the influence of others.

Some of your beliefs may actually end up being values for you, while other beliefs are actually limiting and influencing you in negative ways. Be aware and open to the fact that as I take you through this entire process, you may find that what you have been made to believe has actually limited your thinking and is not a value of yours at all. This can be quite liberating and illuminating.

Now it is time to explore your values through a series of questions to help you begin to articulate them before we dive deeper into what makes them so important and essential to who you are as a person.

What is your personal philosophy on how life should be lived?

_____

_____

_____

_____

What values do you hold dear and believe should never be compromised for any reason?

What are some characteristics or practices of others that you consider undesirable or unacceptable and why?

What do you hope you give to or inspire in others by what you do and say?

What do you need and desire in your life to feel fulfilled and happy?

How have you incorporated your values into how you conduct business and how you work differently from others?

_____
_____
_____
_____
_____

What are your beliefs about how a business should operate or work should be done, and how does this relate to how you think your personal life should also operate?

_____
_____
_____
_____
_____

What are your beliefs that you have been taught and raised to respect?

_____
_____
_____

Take a look at the words you used to describe what you enjoyed and did not enjoy, what makes you who you are, and how you believe you contribute to society in the exercises in Chapter 1. Are there values hidden in these words? If so, note these values here:

_____
_____
_____
_____

Understanding Your Values at the Deepest Level

Now that you have taken time to identify some of your values, it is time to create a Values Mind Map so that you can view them and understand them in a more organized way.

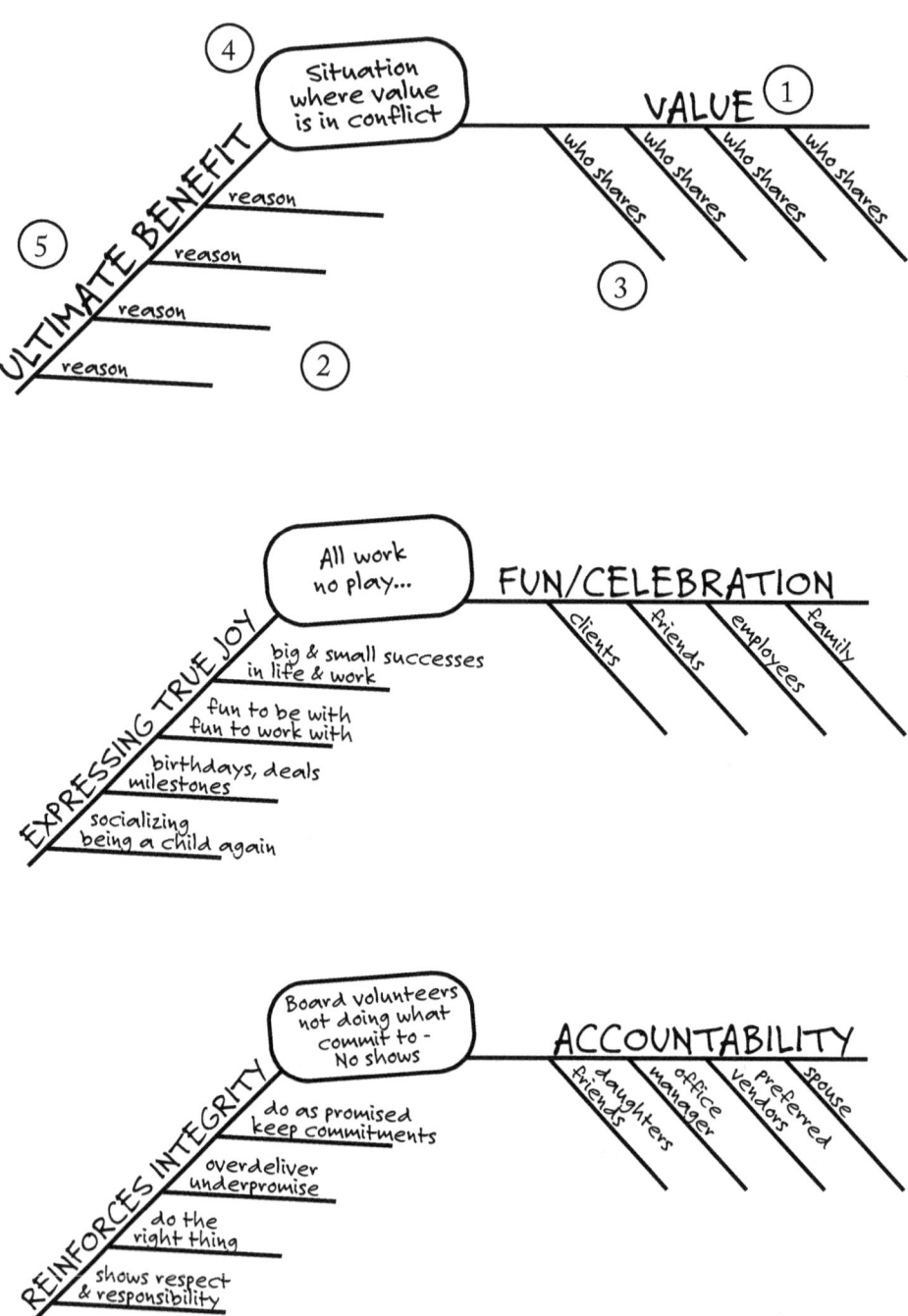

You will build your Mind Map in the following order for each value.
1. **Value:** write the key word or words of your value on the top horizontal line.
2. **Reasons for your value:** on the lines shooting off the diagonal line to the left, write all your reasons for why this value is important to you.
3. **Who shares this value in your life:** draw lines shooting off the line where your value is written and note any specific people (by name) who share this value with you.
4. **How your value may be in conflict or be challenged:** inside the bubble, note a situation or circumstance you may be currently experiencing that is in conflict with this value and potentially causing you stress or discomfort. Only fill this portion in if there is a conflict of some kind currently happening or that has recently occurred.
5. **Ultimate benefit of the value:** on the diagonal line, write the ultimate benefit you will realize from living this value on a daily basis and throughout your life.

The next pages provide an opportunity for you to draft some of your values for mind mapping. However, I encourage you to use the 11 x 17 mind maps sheets you can purchase and download at www.memyselfandinc.com, so you can see all of your values together for better overall analysis and correlative insights.

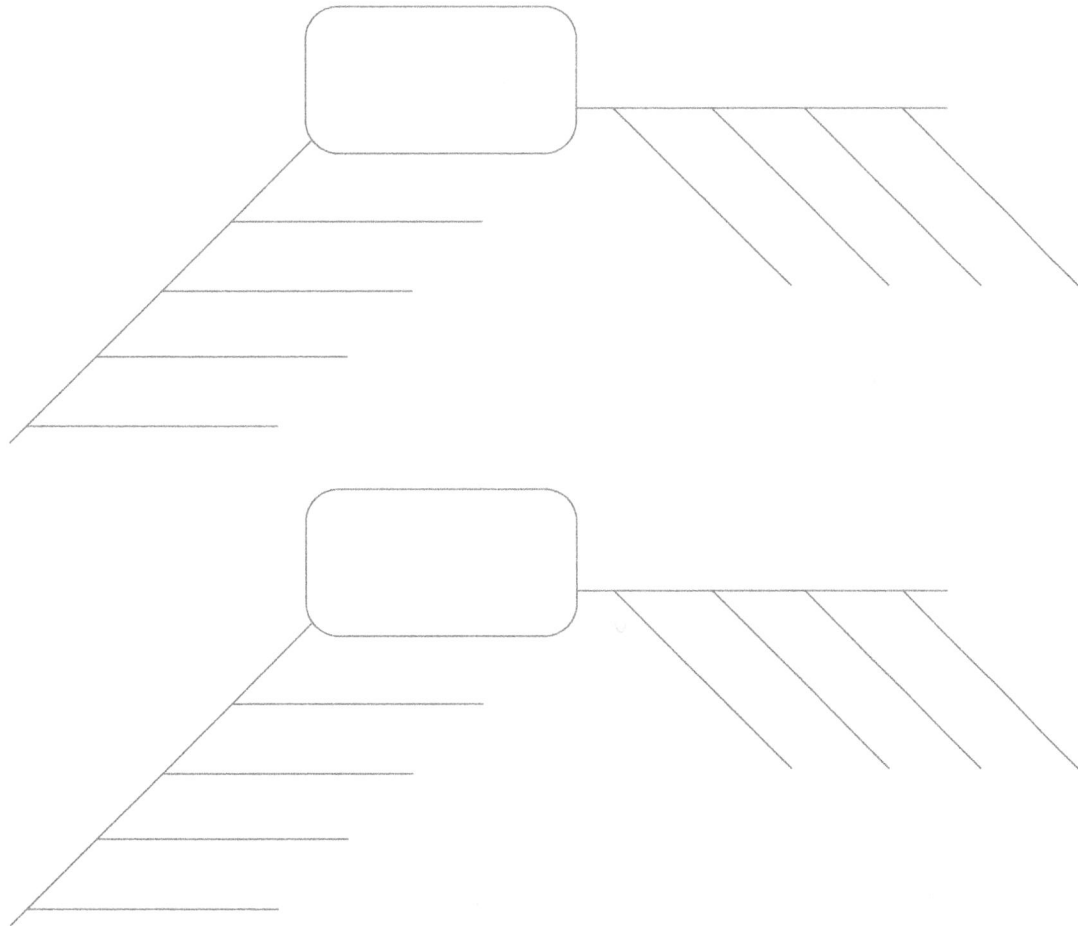

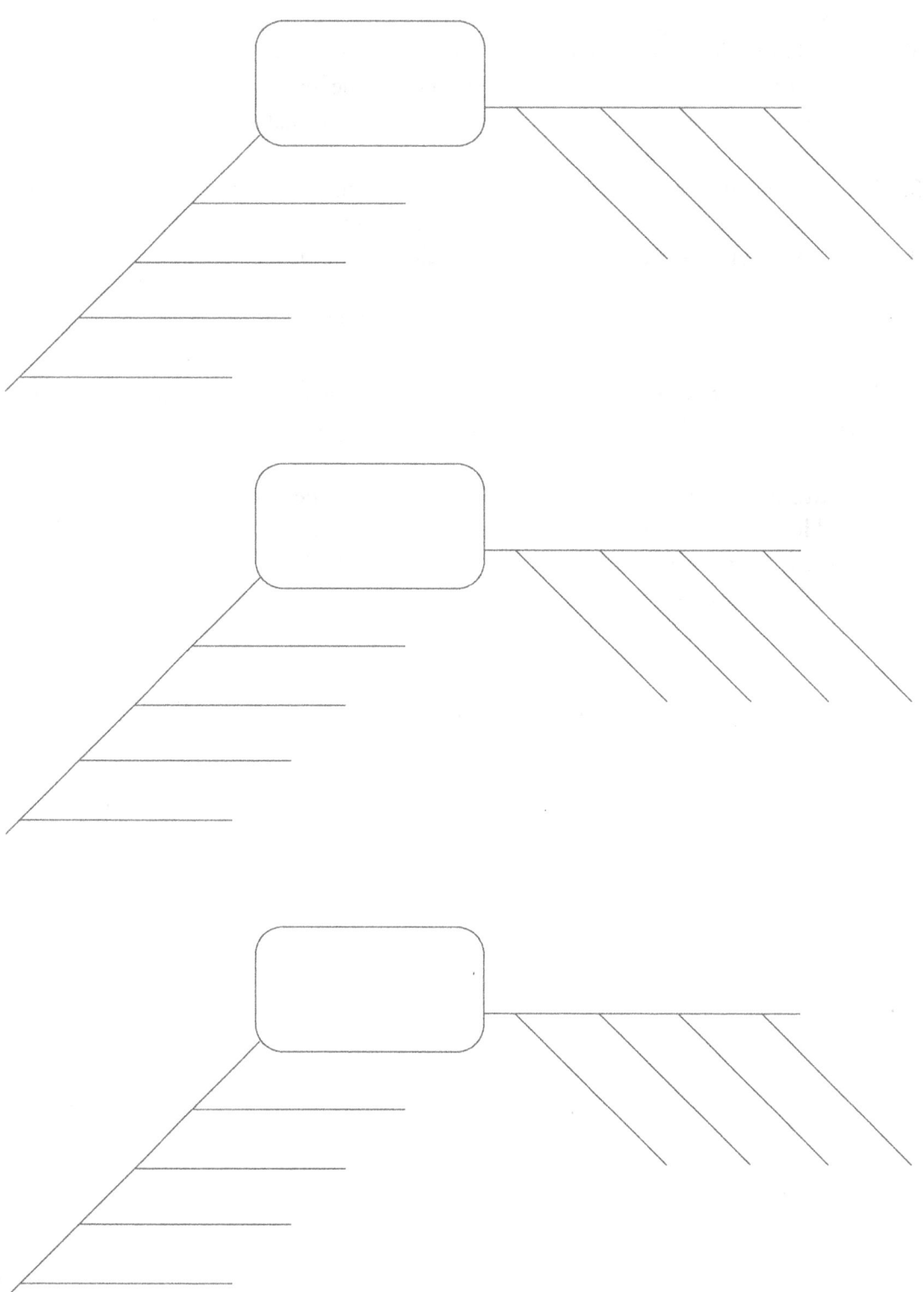

64　From Balance to Synergy

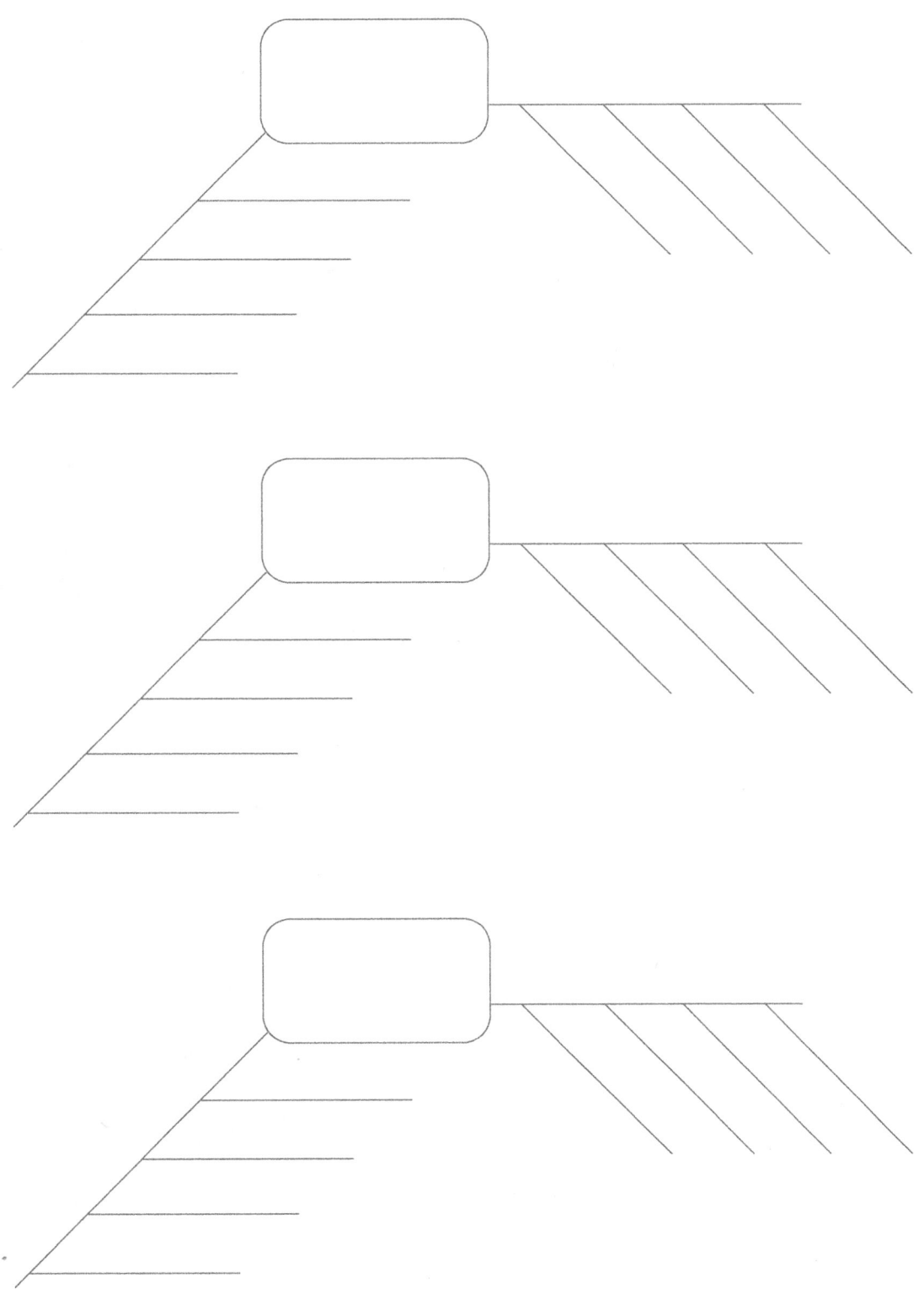

Your Values = Living Your Life

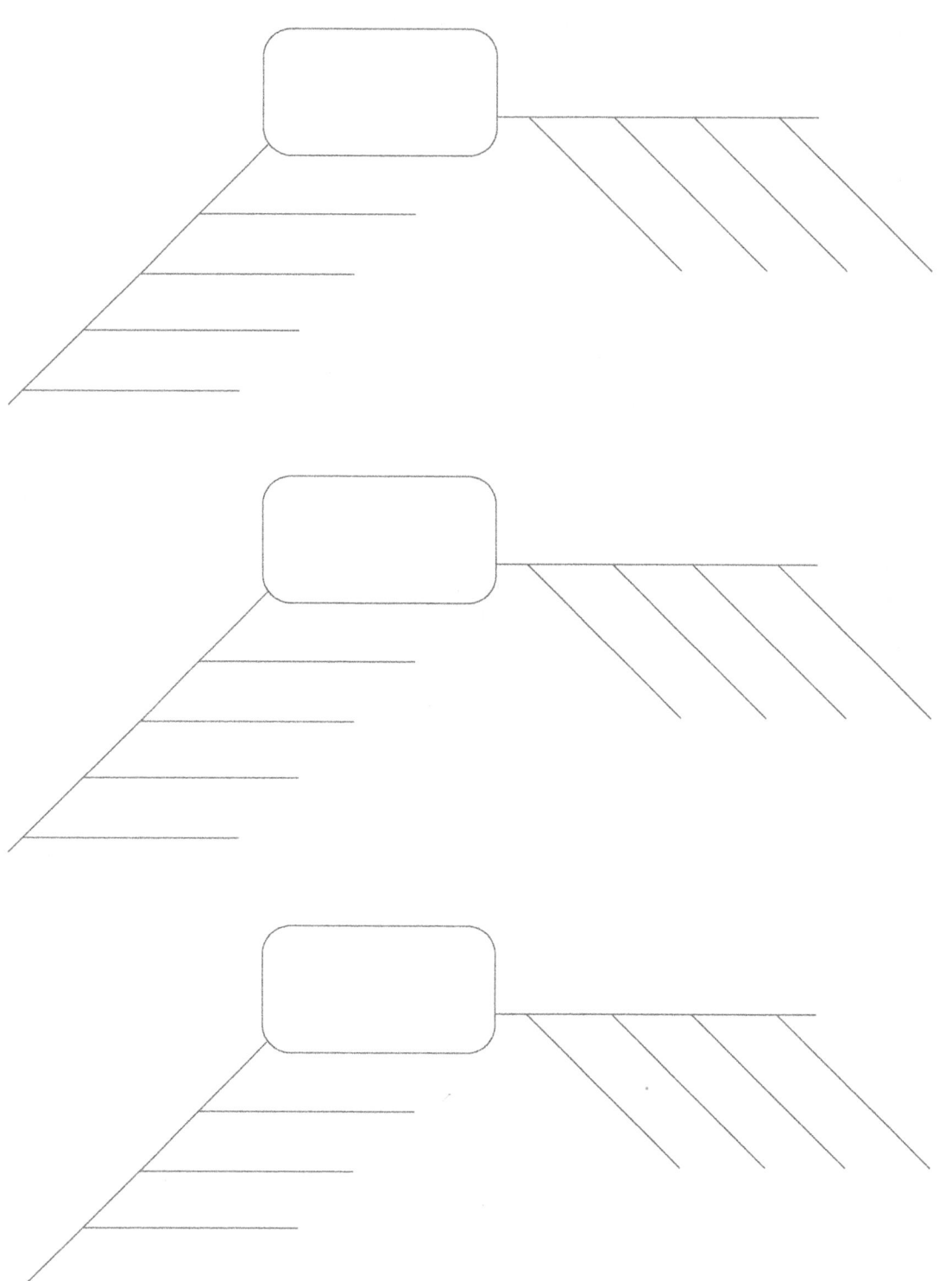

Once captured on your Mind Map, look at your values beyond what they are to what they mean to you. Take a look at why they are important to you and the ultimate benefit you realize from having lived these values as a whole. Identify values that may be in conflict, how they are currently in conflict or are being challenged in some way, and then consider how this is impacting your ability to reach some of your goals.

We will explore this further in the next chapter. Make some additional notes below, based on your review so far.

> Once we realize the power of our thoughts and perceptions, we are enlightened to the probability of achievement versus the possibility of achievement. We become enlightened to the power of goal synergy.

CHAPTER 5
Your Goals = Your Ultimate Life

How do you create synergy in your life? First, you must take a very honest look at what you truly and ultimately believe will make you feel fulfilled, satisfied, and complete in the ME aspect of you, the MYSELF aspect of you, and the INC. aspect of you. This is not as easy as it appears. The entire mindset of opposing forces, conflicting needs, and overwhelming demands has been conditioned into each of our thinking from a very young age.

What gets your heart pumping, your passion flowing, your energy soaring, your metabolism grooving, your mind racing, and your future moving in the right direction? See why understanding your values is so important?

You *must* forget about all of those concerns tugging at your psyche and truly get to the very core of what you really, truly want in your life. Only then can your journey toward synergy begin to blossom and then explode into the amazing life you always hoped could be.

ME Goals, MYSELF Goals, and INC. Goals

The true shift you are now going to make when it comes to setting goals is in looking inside versus outside. Instead of having personal goals and career goals based from a Work/Life Balance perspective, your goals are going to be focused upon the three aspects of YOU. And guess what? Work/Life Balance CANNOT be a goal because as you develop goals to honor the three aspects of you, you will have goals that speak more specifically to each aspect of you to synergize how you live and want to experience your life overall. As I said earlier, the work you do is a part of your life and should not be pitted against it.

Place your Values Mind Map where you can reference it while you do the following exercises. You may find you add a couple of values to your map as you begin to explore your goals.

Go back to your MM&I Quik Quiz (on page 16) and review both what you checked as already enjoying and what you are not fully enjoying. Now you are going to explore some potential goals you could have in each area based on the statements from that Quik Quiz while keeping your values in mind.

ME Goals – Enjoying and Relating with Others

1. I enjoy regular and meaningful interaction with family members. ❏ YES ❏ NO

What would I like to take to another level of interaction with family?

_____
_____
_____
_____

What am I *not* doing that I would like to be doing with family?

_____
_____
_____
_____

2. I enjoy regular and meaningful interaction with friends. ❏ YES ❏ NO

What would I like to take to another level of interaction with friends?

_____
_____
_____
_____

What am I *not* doing that I would like to be doing with friends?

_____
_____
_____
_____

3. I enjoy meaningful and intimate interaction with a spouse or significant other.
❏ YES ❏ NO

> What would I like to take to another level of interaction with my spouse or significant other?
>
> _____
> _____
> _____
> _____
>
> What am I *not* doing that I would like to be doing with my spouse or significant other?
>
> _____
> _____
> _____
> _____

4. I enjoy and explore my community with my friends, family, spouse, or significant other.
❏ YES ❏ NO

> What would I like to take to another level of interaction and exploration within my community?
>
> _____
> _____
> _____
>
> What am I *not* doing that I would like to be doing within my community?
>
> _____
> _____
> _____

MYSELF Goals – Embracing and Being YOU

5. I make it a priority to allocate time for myself on a regular basis, so I can recharge, refocus, and relax. ❏ YES ❏ NO

What am I doing that I would like to take to another level or do more often for myself?

_____
_____
_____
_____

What am I *not* doing that I would like to be doing for myself?

_____
_____
_____

6. I have hobbies or things I like to do just for me and my own self-expression, self-development, and fulfillment. ❏ YES ❏ NO

What hobbies or things am I doing that I would like to take to another level or do more often?

_____
_____
_____

What hobbies or things am I *not* doing that I would like to be doing?

_____
_____
_____

7. I believe that taking care of me is a priority; therefore, I regularly exercise and eat right to nourish my mind, spirit, and being. ❑ YES ❑ NO

   What am I doing to take care of myself that I would like to take to another level or do more often?

   _____
   _____
   _____

   What am I *not* doing to take care of myself that I would like to be doing?

   _____
   _____
   _____

8. I enjoy and regularly learn new things and explore new ideas or places alone and with others as a way of continually bringing more to my life and my work. ❑ YES ❑ NO

   What am I doing to learn new things or explore new ideas that I would like to take to another level or do more often?

   _____
   _____
   _____

   What am I *not* learning or exploring that I would like to be doing?

   _____
   _____
   _____
   _____

INC. Goals – Contributing to a Profession or Society and Making a Difference

9. I look forward to going to work each day and cannot wait to see what the day brings in both challenges and opportunities. ❑ YES ❑ NO

    What am I doing that I would like to take to another level or do more often at work?

    _____
    _____
    _____
    _____

    What am I *not* doing at work that I would like to be doing?

    _____
    _____
    _____

10. I believe that I am doing exactly what I was meant to do as a profession and get great satisfaction from the work that I do. ❑ YES ❑ NO

    What am I doing that I believe is what I was meant to be doing and would like to take to another level or do more often?

    _____
    _____
    _____

    What am I *not* doing that I would like to be doing for greater satisfaction in my work?

    _____
    _____
    _____

11. I gain great satisfaction and inspiration from the people I work with and do business with who reinforce that the work I do makes a difference. ❑ YES ❑ NO

   What am I doing with others at work that I would like to take to another level or do more often?

   _____

   _____

   _____

   _____

   What am I *not* doing that I would like to be doing with others in my work?

   _____

   _____

   _____

12. I have developed friendships through work that are meaningful and valued, but I also have a network of friends outside of work that is stimulating and important in my life.
   ❑ YES ❑ NO

   What friendships inside and outside of work would I like to take to another level or develop more?

   _____

   _____

   _____

   _____

   What am I *not* doing to develop friendships at work or could be doing to nurture friendships?

   _____

   _____

   _____

Capturing Your Goals to Synergize Your Life

It is now time to create a Goals Mind Map so that you can analyze your goals from deep within to know truly what you want and don't want to achieve.

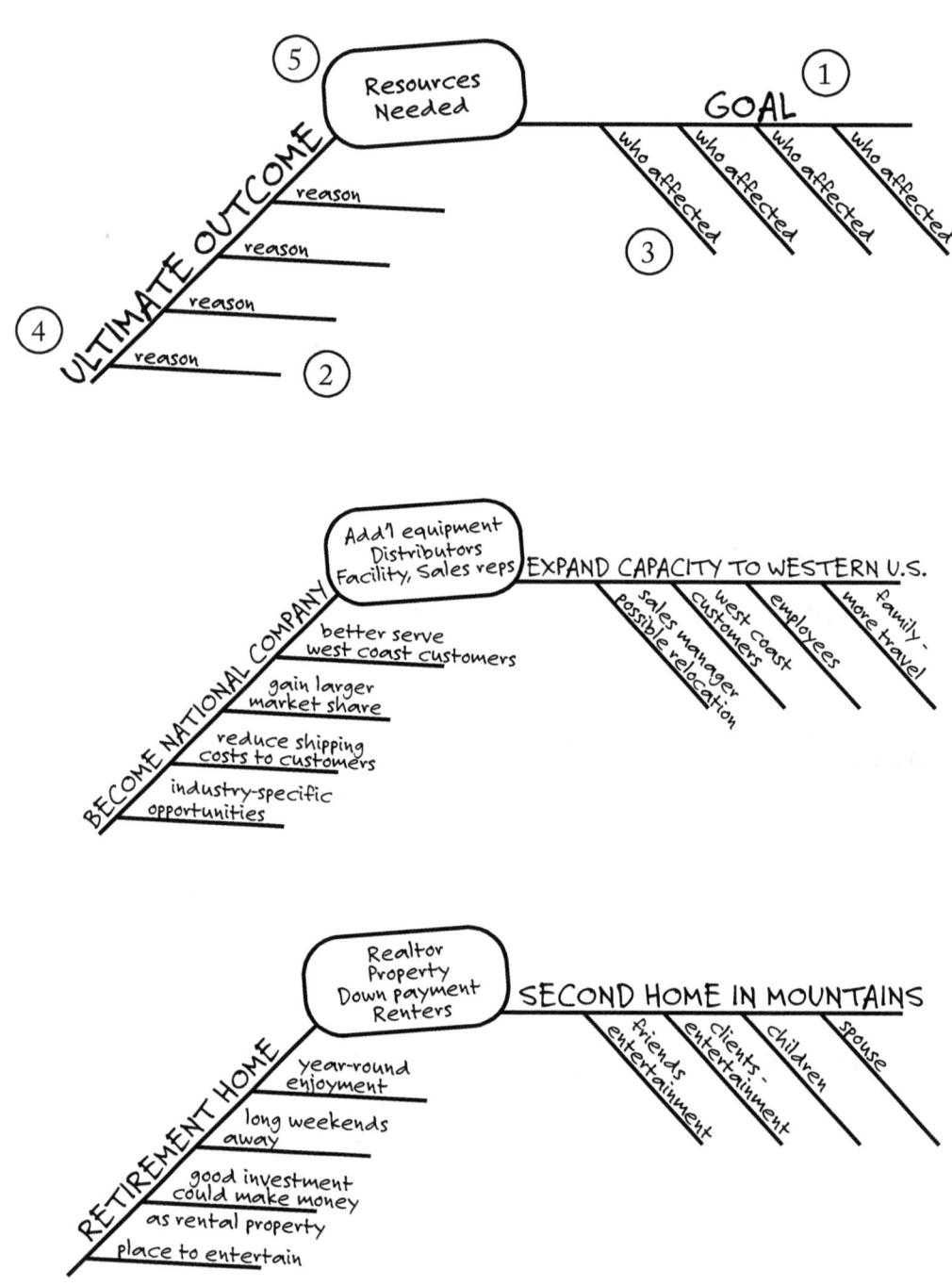

(example values for reference)

You will build your Mind Map in the following order for each goal.

1. **Goal:** a couple of words that express the goal on the top horizontal line.

2. **Reasons for your goal:** on the lines shooting out from the diagonal line, note all the reasons this goal is important to you or someone else for you to achieve.

3. **Individuals affected by the goal:** drawing lines underneath the goal line, write the names of people who will be impacted or affected by the goal. They may benefit from you achieving it. They may also not benefit. They may be necessary or instrumental for you to reach this goal. If someone is going to be impacted in any way, write their names down.

4. **Expected outcome once goal is reached:** on the diagonal line, write what will ultimately be the outcome of you reaching that goal.

5. **Resources needed to achieve the goal:** inside the bubble, note what is needed to make the goal a reality from your perspective.

Write anything and everything that comes to mind, no matter how crazy, insignificant, dreamy, positive, or negative it seems. Get it all down. Most important is capturing *all* the reasons for each of your goals. This cannot be emphasized enough. If you are really being honest and disclosing all that you ultimately want or think that you want and why, you will begin to see some things in a brand new way. You will begin to see for the first time where your mind's eye begins, your heart's desire beats, and where other influences have made their marks in shifting your focus away from what you truly want to achieve.

Once you have completed your mind mapping, put your map down, walk away for a moment, and then go back and look at it. Really look at it. Keep looking and adding ideas until you simply cannot think of another thing to add.

With both your Values Mind Map and your Goals Mind Map, you will find that you will think of things to add to the reasons, another value, or another goal. Don't limit or sensor. This is extremely important. Carry both with you for several days and glance at them and add as you are inspired to add more to them.

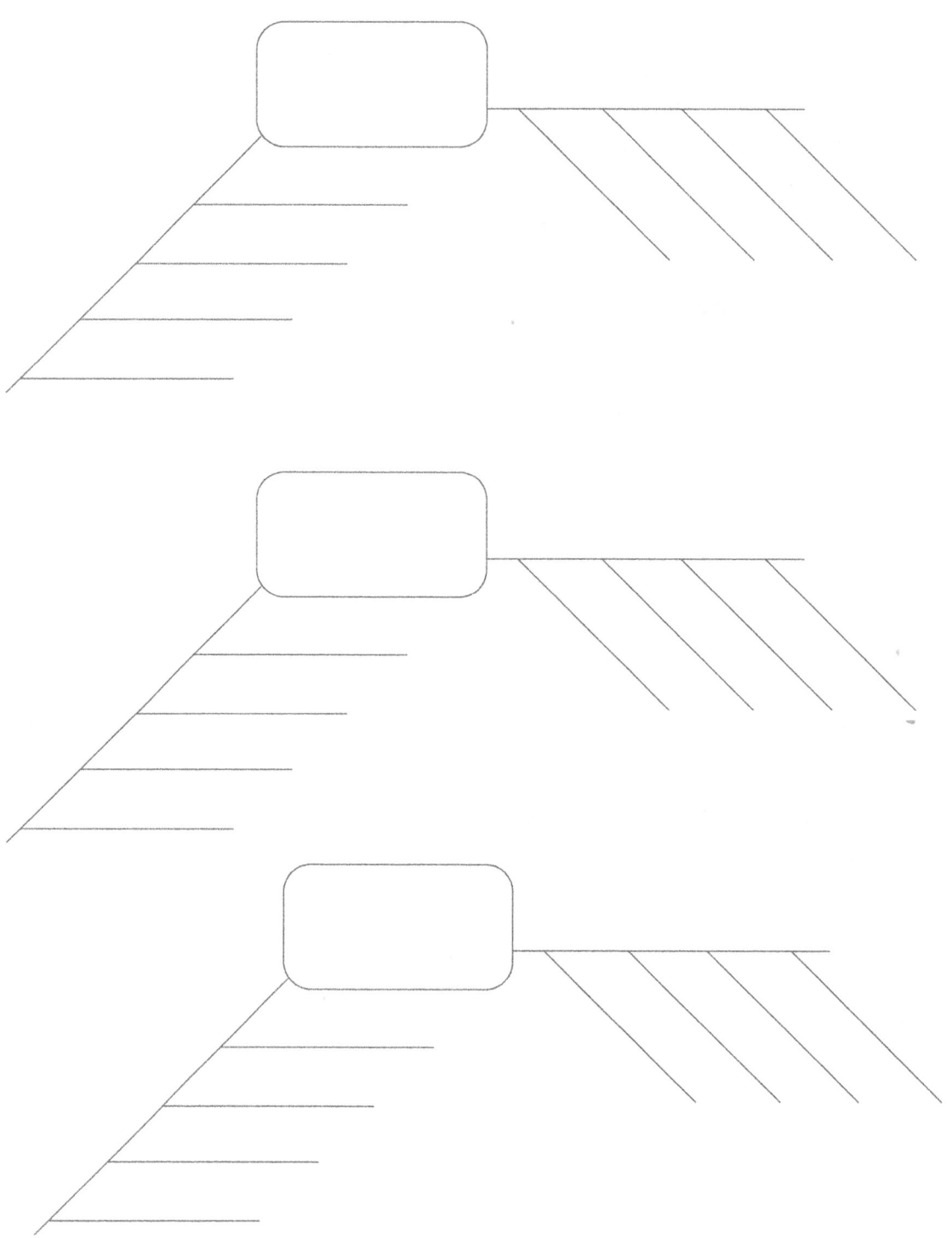

"The reason that balance is so impossible is that many of us are trying to balance aspects of our lives that aren't even a part of who we are or who we want to be. We are taking actions based on what someone else thinks we should be or wants us to be."

CHAPTER 6
Whose Goals Are They?

In the last chapter, we captured all of our goals: our ME goals, our MYSELF goals, and our INC. goals. Putting them all out there in our mind-mapping universe allowed us to see them as a whole instead of as separate galaxies. We wrote them down. We recorded why we have them, no matter how silly or valid the reasons. We recorded what we expect from them, no matter how simple or grandiose the expectations. And we identified those individuals who might be affected if we reached them, as well as individuals whose involvement is needed in order to reach them.

Are you feeling overwhelmed? Are you feeling as though there is no way you can accomplish these goals all together? Of course you feel that way now. You are still in a Work/Life Balance way of thinking. Have faith and keep moving through this process.

When I first took this new approach to analyzing my goals, I made another discovery. The reason why balance is so impossible is that many of us are trying to balance aspects of our lives that aren't even part of who we are or what want to be. We are taking action based on what *someone else* thinks we should be or wants us to be. It is no wonder we feel conflict, opposing forces, and other negative emotions. It is no wonder that, as a result of this turmoil within, and without us even realizing it, we sabotage and impede our ability to have balance. Quite simply, subconsciously we are not sure these are aspects of our lives that we really want to balance. We are not motivated to achieve goals that were never really ours anyway.

In this chapter, you are going to begin exploring the whole idea of whom these goals really belong to. You will start to prioritize your goals and weed out those that are in the hearts of others, not your own. Through this process, you can completely and honestly analyze your goals.

By the time you have gone through the exercises, you will know whether they are: 1) your goals; 2) goals you think you should have; or 3) goals that have been imposed upon you by society, a loved one, or some other influencing faction. Then you can eliminate, without guilt, the goals that are not truly yours and focus entirely on those exciting goals that make you ready to take on the world.

The first goals that you need to analyze are those that appear to not be entirely yours alone. The reason I use the word "appear" is because you should not dismiss a goal as invalid just because someone wants you to achieve it. This could still be a very real goal for you.

Someone else having that goal for you or along with you doesn't necessarily mean you can't embrace it. The key is to determine whether their involvement or desire is a catalyst or a roadblock, an inspiration or a deterrent, a confidence builder or a confidence buster.

List any goals below in which someone else has influenced you or would also like to see you reach this goal.

_____
_____
_____
_____

List any goals that you have repeated year after year and have not made much progress in achieving.

_____
_____
_____
_____

Now I want you to begin by looking at your goals that have an outcome that will directly impact or rely on someone else to achieve. You are now going to dig a little deeper to the core of the "why" and "what for" in regard to your goals. Make notes about the following three areas: happiness, pride, and expectations.

The happiness trap: Will achieving this goal make you happier than you are right at this very moment? How and why will it make you happier?

_____
_____
_____
_____

Your ultimate happiness: *If you did not achieve this goal, would you be unhappy with your life? Would not reaching this goal make it difficult for you to enjoy your life? Why?*

_____
_____
_____
_____

Someone else's ultimate happiness: *Does this goal hinge on making someone else in your life happy? If the goal is not achieved, will this person be unhappy with the outcome or unhappy with you? Why?*

_____
_____
_____
_____

The pride trap: Will achieving this goal make you proud of the accomplishment for yourself and others? If so, how and in what way does this affect the outcome?

_____
_____
_____
_____

Your sense of pride: *Are you doing it for you and you alone? Do you want this goal to prove something to yourself so that you can be proud that you achieved it against the odds? Why?*

_____
_____
_____
_____

Someone else's sense of pride: *Are you going for this goal to make someone else proud of you? Why is this important? Will you feel like you have let them down if you do not achieve it? Will you think that they will think less of you if you do not achieve it? Why?*

_____

_____

_____

_____

The expectation trap: Do you feel an expectation to achieve this goal? Where did this expectation come from?

_____

_____

_____

_____

Your expectation: *Is this an expectation you determined on your own? If so, is it one you consider a desired challenge, or is it something you just want to achieve so that you can move on to something else? Why?*

_____

_____

_____

_____

Someone else's expectation for you: *Was this expectation imposed upon you by someone else? Do you now feel obligated because you do not want to let this person down? Why?*

_____

_____

_____

_____

Valid or invalid: Hopefully, as a result of this exercise, you will begin to see which goals are truly yours and which goals are ultimately someone else's that you simply adopted out of a sense of obligation, pride, or to make others happy.

Based on your assessment of happiness, pride, and expectations, which goals are still a valid goal for you?

_____
_____
_____

Are You a Goal Imposer?

Another issue to review involves answering the following questions to better understand other aspects about your goals. Those of us who are very goals-oriented naturally find ourselves with goals for others, both in our personal lives and at work. Also, because we are *so* goals-oriented, we tend to be somewhat intimidating to others. Without even realizing it, we may create in others a compulsion to please us in theit lives or to advance in their jobs, resulting in an environment of guilt and dissatisfaction that we are not even aware is occurring.

Which of *your* goals are *you* imposing on others? Is this a goal you have identified to also be a goal for a specific person because it is necessary to have them involved for you to reach your goal?

_____
_____
_____
_____

Which of your goals rely on someone else in order to be accomplished? Is the other person aware that your goal is dependent on him or her?

_____
_____
_____
_____

Most critical, in either case, has the other person embraced this goal as his or her own, knowing that it is key to you reaching your goal – or are they reluctantly accepting the goal because of a sense of obligation, a desire for job security, or a fear of disappointing you? Make some notes of thoughts related to this.

_____

_____

_____

_____

I have fallen into the trap of being the goal imposer, even though I had quite effectively weeded out those goals that were not really mine. While I had already begun realizing a much more synergized existence (as a result of no longer being victim to others' expectations), I discovered I was potentially sabotaging my own efforts by imposing expectations on others. As the goal imposer, I had to come to terms with this reality: I needed to look for alternative ways to meet my own goals whenever the goal I imposed was not embraced by the other person. The best part is, once I did this, other goals that were much more synergistic in other areas complementary to my own came to light. Open-mindedness and acceptance were absolutely critical to my being able to move forward into real action – for everyone concerned.

Changing or Eliminating Goals

Now that you have assessed all your goals that involve other people, it is time to review them again honestly and intentionally.

Can you eliminate some of these goals or reevaluate them to make them your own? If yes, note these goals to be potentially rewritten or eliminated below.

_____

_____

_____

_____

Chances are that this is getting a bit uncomfortable because eliminating these goals will in turn affect others in the process. Don't be afraid to be honest with yourself and others by simply saying a particular goal is not one you have a passion for. Those who really matter in your life will support you. Those who don't and try to make you feel guilty are not the type of people you need in your life anyway. I know because as a result of coming to these realizations, I made significant changes in my life to eliminate all those "others" who were draining me emotionally and affecting my ability to focus on what would help me synergize my life, including clients, vendors, and fair-weather friends. You can do the same.

Before completely eliminating the goals you identified in the previous exercise, could a goal become more of your own by changing the focus based on what is important to you based on your values? If yes, note how the goal could be modified to speak to you personally and passionately.

___

___

___

___

Action Steps to Set Yourself FREE: Note below some action steps you are going to take to eliminate goals. This could include conversations you will have with others or exploring options to make the goal more meaningful for you before eliminating.

1.
2.
3.
4.
5.
6.
7.
8.
9.
10.

> Why does conflict exist in our lives? Because whatever the conflicts may be, they are typically going against what we believe, value, or stand for. Sometimes we don't exactly know what it is, but we know it does not feel right.

CHAPTER 7
Aligning Values and Goals

We are going to dive even deeper into the correlation between your values and your goals and why it is so important that they are in alignment. Pull out your Values Mind Map sheet or go to the pages where your Values Mind Map is located in this workbook.

Now you are going to prioritize your values to better understand yourself and why you react the way that you do in given circumstances. I warn you, this is not going to be easy. It will seem hard at first to make one value appear more important than another. However, as you really think about them and start to see the priorities take shape, you will begin to understand so much about yourself. I guarantee it.

If you get stuck, consider the following points to help you prioritize:

- **Place a star "★" or an asterisk "✳" next to those values where you will make absolutely no exceptions.** Regardless of circumstance, these values hold strong and true, and you will not waver from them. They are that important to you. These values are nonnegotiable aspects of you.

- **Place a check mark "✔" next to any value where you can be flexible and waver slightly.** It is still important; however, you allow some leeway. An example for me is my value of accountability and respecting people's time. It is important to me in how I behave; however, I accept that not everyone is that way. And specifically, with some loved ones who are notoriously late, I have grown to accept it and have not eliminated them from my life as a result. Interestingly, however, I have eliminated people who did not respect my time as a client or a vendor. So that says to me that it is still important enough to influence my decisions.

- **Mark nothing next to the remaining values (without a star, asterisk, or checkmark).** They were important enough to write down; however, they do not necessarily guide your everyday existence or way of doing things. They are nice to have as values, and you feel they are part of you to some extent.

Now that you have done the above, start prioritizing starting with the number 1 and then so on focusing on the values with stars. Then move to the values with a checkmark and prioritize them starting with the letter A and so on. The values with nothing next to them, simply leave as is.

Values in Conflict: Look at your top values. Now look at some of the goals you are trying to accomplish. Are any aspects of these values not being honored that are impacting your ability to make progress with your goals?

Make notes about this below. Also add those conflicts to the corresponding value in your Values Mind Map.

_____
_____
_____
_____

Goals Affected/Impacted: Now look at your goals and the people who may be impacted, influenced, are necessary to help you achieve, or will benefit from achieving that goal. Are people listed who don't share some of your values, especially your nonnegotiable ones? List these people here along with the goal that is being affected.

Goal	Don't Share Value	Do Share Value

Goals Shifted: Review the goals you determined in the previous chapter should shift in focus based on your initial review of your Values Mind Map. Now look at your values priorities and determine if the goal still is shifted to be meaningful to you. Also, is there something more to be added or shifted about the goal as a result of knowing your priorities more explicitly?

_____
_____
_____
_____

Goals Added: Based on your priorities and insights gained thus far, would you like to add any goals? If so, list them below, and then add them to your Goals Mind Map, completing all components of the mind mapping process for additional insight.

_____
_____
_____
_____

Goals Eliminated: While you may have already eliminated some goals based on the previous chapter's exercises, are there any other goals you realize are just not something you are passionate about or important to you based on your prioritized values? List them below and then mark a big "X" through them on your Goals Mind Map.

_____
_____
_____
_____

You have just given yourself permission to only focus on what matters to you, for you, and to those you care most about. Doesn't that feel great?

> Everything in your life begins and ends with you. Accept that this is true and then realize that it really is about the mindset you operate from each and every day. If your thinking is holding you back, then it's time for a new way of thinking.

SECTION 2

Three Promises – Rewiring Your Thinking

My grandmother, affectionately known as Granny Pea, was a huge influence in my life. Through her love and encouragement, she instilled in me that I could do anything I set my mind to do. When you step outside of your comfort zone, it can seem a bit daunting. That's when having some mantras to keep you charging forward helps defray some of the doubts that will naturally enter into your mind, especially when you have been brainwashed into thinking it is about balance instead of synergy.

It was in my early adulthood that I truly began to understand and embrace three mantras, or promises, that my grandmother instilled in me as I continued to grow and tried to achieve various things. These three promises are:

PROMISE #1: I will find a way or make a way by helping others find a way or make a way.

PROMISE #2: I will not feel guilty about making life easier for myself.

PROMISE #3: I will be open to all possible resources, options, and support.

This section will help you explore the power these three promises can represent in helping rewire your thinking to a synergy mindset.

> "None of us can achieve what we ultimately seek to achieve without others being involved in some way, shape, or form. Through helping others, we help ourselves in ways that may not seem apparent at the time, yet are profound in hindsight."

CHAPTER 8
Find a Way or Make a Way

PROMISE #1: I will find a way or make a way by helping others find a way or make a way.

When you set out to find a way or make a way, you are giving yourself permission to succeed. You have such passion that whatever you are striving to achieve does not seem insurmountable. At first glance, this statement could be taken out of context, if you only look at the first part of the phrase and don't take into consideration the helping of others. "Find a way or make a way" can easily be misconstrued as quite selfish and self-centered. So let's get something straight right now: this promise is about determination and forging forward toward your goals, but not at the expense or detriment to anyone or anything. You must also make the agreement with yourself that you will be impeccable in your actions and live up to your word at all times.

In finding a way or making a way, it will be more about paying attention to opportunities, keeping your mind open to the possibilities, and having the tenacity not to be discouraged in the face of disappointment, challenges, unexpected turns, and delays.

Key to this promise is an underlying sense of unity with others. This is where the ME, the MYSELF, and the INC. aspects of you can and should be turned full piston on in how you show up each day. Why? Because the reality is that we need others just as they need us to accomplish what we ultimately desire to accomplish.

Look at your Values Mind Map and consider with whom you share the same values. Make some notations below of these people as they relate to your goals. You may even find that some of these same people who share a particular value also will be impacted or benefit from you reaching your goal.

_____

_____

_____

_____

Whom should you add to a particular goal because they share a value that resonates with that particular goal? Note them here and then add them as another person related to that goal on your mind map. They could end up being an unexpected yet delightfully valuable resource.

MM&I MOMENT OF INSPIRATION

"Your self perspective can either propel your progress or pause your power."

- Sherré DeMao -

> "We as a society seem to like making things harder on ourselves as a required rite of passage toward earning a goal or achievement. We need to stop working so hard at working hard."

CHAPTER 9
Don't Feel Guilty about Making Life Easier for Yourself

PROMISE #2: I will not feel guilty about making life easier for myself.

This is probably the toughest one of all to follow. Some of us may think that if we don't do something entirely on our own, then we somehow have not earned it quite as purely or valiantly. Many of us have heard that you must work hard to be successful, and while this is true to a certain extent, we don't have to work as hard at working hard.

What do I mean by this? Quite simply, we need to take a step back every now and again and ask ourselves if there is an easier way to achieve the same end result in whatever stage we are in while working toward our goal. Making a task or step in the process easier for ourselves is not slacking or taking a shortcut; it's just plain smart. Why work harder when you can work smarter, more efficiently, or have help along the way?

What are some things you are doing that you feel could be done more efficiently by someone else or simplified in some way? Don't worry about not having the solutions; just make a note of what you think right now.

_____

_____

_____

_____

Who could be helping you whom you are not allowing to help you? What kind of a skill do you wish you had, or someone had, to help you do what you are trying to do more effectively? How could you get something done that you want to get done with help from someone else?

_____
_____
_____

Another aspect of making life easier on ourselves is not to take so many things so personally and not to jump to conclusions. How many times do we catch ourselves worrying about things that never happen because we make assumptions? How many times do we undermine our own ability to continue during a setback because we take whatever happened so personally instead of simply learning from the situation so as to make it easier the next go around?

What assumptions are you making that are keeping you from getting the help you need?

_____
_____
_____

What do you honestly believe is a hindrance in making things easier for yourself?

_____
_____
_____

Once you truly make a conscious effort to ask yourself how something can be accomplished more easily, or how you can make your life easier to deal with, you will open yourself completely to being able to adhere to synergy and the promise of making life easier for yourself.

MM&I MOMENT OF INSPIRATION

"Your ability to move what you desire forward is always in your hands, in your heart, and in your mind."

- Sherré DeMao -

> "How open-minded are you ... really? Many people who perceive themselves to be open-minded hinder their abilities to reach their goals because they are not engaging synergy in full motion."

CHAPTER 10
Being Open to All Possible Resources, Options, and Support

PROMISE #3: I will be open to all possible resources, options, and support.

What is most important to remember with this promise is that you must be open to support and resources from unexpected places. This is where people who have synergized their lives are strides ahead of others. They understand that a means of support or a resource they could use may very well come from somewhere out of nowhere and could be missed if not open to its potential. You could also have a means of support or a resource literally under your nose, and for some reason, it has been discarded or not even considered due to some obscure belief or perception that holds you back from seeing it as an opportunity.

Probably the most important aspect of being open to all possible resources and support is that by doing so, you are also following promises #1 and #2. You will be finding a way or making a way, and you will also be making life easier for yourself in the process. Now doesn't this sound like a much more exciting way to move forward toward your goals than how you were operating before?

What people have found as they have put these three promises into action is that they are in a better place to be at their best at all times. Being and doing your best is something that those of us who are goals-driven strive for on a daily basis. The reality is that sometimes we don't feel so hot. Then what? Well, then that is when having resources or support helps us still do our best when we are perhaps not at our best. Now that is synergy in motion!

Go back and look at all of your goals and inside the bubbles where you noted what is needed to help you achieve that goal. Write all the notes you made here below.

_____

_____

_____

_____

Now, glancing through these notes above, write down any assumptions, limitations, or challenges you believe are keeping you from having these resources, options, or support right now.

_____
_____
_____
_____

The next two sections are going to help you overcome what you believe may be limiting you.

MM&I MOMENT OF INSPIRATION

"If you feel you must sacrifice, then you are in a limiting state of mind that is hindering your true potential to succeed."

- Sherré DeMao -

> So many people are on the cusp of their greatness or happiness but are not able to get there because they believe the situation is out of their control or simply is the way that it is. They wish things could be different, yet they don't believe there is anything that they can do to change it.

SECTION 3

Wishful Thinking: From If Only to Absolutely!

If only, if only, if only … Have you caught yourself saying this out loud or wishfully to yourself? If only … if only … if only!

If only I had more confidence? If only I had more choices or options? If only I had fewer choices or options? If only I had more money? If only I had more time? If only I had more support?

Wishing, while fun to do on a birthday cake before blowing out candles, is complacent. It is a reaction to the circumstance or events happening to you, wishing they were different or that something will miraculously happen to make them different. Wishful thinking oftentimes focuses on what is wrong versus what is right. Wishing tends to focus on fixing something in the present or wishing to immediately fill something that is missing.

Which type of thinker are you? Wishful or hopeful? This section will help you understand your wishful thinking so that you can make hope your new emotional pathway toward synergy, which will be further explored in Chapter 23.

> Our passion feeds our faith in ourselves and in what we are doing. When you are passionate about something, it is a part of you so completely that you simply believe. Call it blind faith; it is confidence in its purest sense.

CHAPTER 11
If Only I Had More Confidence

You may have already begun to get a clue about what may be undermining your confidence. However, answer these questions to further explore what could be affecting your confidence, so you can begin to overcome and reignite your hope, faith, passion, optimism, and belief in who you are and what you are doing.

Where do you lack confidence in what you are doing? Where does this lack of confidence stem from?

_____

_____

_____

_____

Do the areas in which you lack confidence also coincide with areas that you simply are not passionate about or don't know enough about? If so, then why are you spending so much time in these areas? Is there someone else who could take this role so you can focus on where your passion lies? Is there training or some aspect of learning that you could gain that will help you build confidence if it is essential to your success?

_____

_____

_____

_____

Take a look at your values. How can these answers help you in evaluating your areas where you lack confidence? Are some of your values being challenged in a way that is undermining your efforts?

_____
_____
_____
_____

List all the people in your life with whom you interact on a daily or regular basis. Be totally honest and note how they are a positive influence or a negative one and why. Note also if they challenge you and if it is in a good way or a demeaning way. If there are those in regular contact with you who are highly negative or draining your confidence, how can you reduce or eliminate your interaction with them? Do they realize they are being negative, and can this possibly be averted so that they can become a positive influence?

_____
_____
_____
_____
_____
_____
_____

MM&I MOMENT OF INSPIRATION

"Leaps of faith always begin with a belief in yourself followed by action, which are then blessed by divine directives that catapult your possibilities into probabilities."

- Sherré DeMao

> "The most effective people are managers of their destinies. They know how to get things done beyond the confines of their minds or capabilities, and as a result, make better choices when decisions need to be made."

CHAPTER 12
If Only I Had More Choices, Fewer Choices

Do you have a lot of irons in the fire? Are there several things or projects you have started with none of them really progressing? List them and then answer these questions.

_____
_____
_____
_____

Which of these current projects will most directly help you achieve your goals?

_____
_____
_____
_____

Which of these projects will impact your bottom line with increased profit or greater income?

_____
_____
_____
_____

Which of these projects will help you perform more effectively to free up you or others to focus on other things in the long term?

_____
_____
_____

Which ones started out with gusto and then fizzled? Why did this happen? Has something changed that now makes them not so appealing, or did something roadblock their progress?

_____
_____
_____

Which ones will have a direct impact in the most immediate way when completed toward your goals?

_____
_____
_____

Are there things you know you need to get finished or to get started in order to take something in your life to the next level, but you cannot seem to find the time or ability to focus? List them here and answer these questions.

_____
_____
_____

What is the reason these things have not been started or progress has stopped?

_____
_____
_____
_____

What are the next phases needed to take it one step further?

_____
_____
_____
_____

Who or what could move them forward for you?

_____
_____
_____
_____

"Where we've gone astray is in thinking that money is the end all to achievement and success. As a result, we are too focused on making money because we equate it with a measure of our wealth. What it really takes is leveraging all of our resources."

CHAPTER 13
If Only I Had More Money

What exactly are your attitudes about money that could be affecting your ability to identify or leverage other resources?

Answer these questions to gain an understanding of how you view money as a whole. Chances are you have never really thought about this before, so it will be enlightening to discover why you approach money the way you do.

When you hear the word money, what first comes to mind?

_____
_____
_____

How did you view money growing up? How was money depicted to you by your parents and family? Plentiful? Limited? Never Enough? Elaborate as much as possible.

_____
_____
_____
_____

Are you a saver or a spender? Why?

_____
_____
_____

Where does money fall currently in your stress scale? High? Low? Why?

_____
_____
_____
_____

Are you a bargain shopper, or do you buy only the best, with money being no object? Or are you somewhere in between? Why do you think you are this way?

_____
_____
_____
_____

What is your idea of a good value for your money? What is your idea of wasting money?

_____
_____
_____
_____

Whom do you admire in how they handle money and why?

_____
_____
_____
_____

Your INC. Aspect of YOU

Now it is time to help you get beyond money being your only answer. Here are some questions to help you open your mind to other resources you can tap into at work.

Is there money not being made because you or others are being pulled away from income-generating activity? Take a look at these nonincome activities and brainstorm ways for these tasks to be done using technology or other people.

_____
_____
_____
_____

How could technology help you serve customers better, operate more efficiently, simplify a function, or elevate a service or product offering for competitive advantage?

_____
_____
_____
_____

What are you doing internally that may be better served by outsourcing it to other people?

_____
_____
_____

How can you better use other people's time to engage them in the support of your work efforts?

_____
_____
_____
_____

What are some needs in your business or position that seem out of reach at the moment? Could they be attainable through bartering or sharing with someone?

_____
_____
_____

Your ME and MYSELF Aspect of YOU

Here are some questions to help you open your mind to other resources you can leverage in all other areas of your life.

How can you leverage the time of others in your household to gain more time for yourself?

_____
_____
_____
_____

Where can technology be used to simplify your life at home?

_____
_____
_____
_____

Who can you share expenses or services with to gain a better rate?

_____
_____
_____
_____

Who can you potentially trade services with such as house sitting, lawn care, or babysitting to gain more money for other things or more time for yourself? Remember that it does not have to be the same service.

_____
_____
_____
_____

Whom do you know who owns something that you would like, who in return would enjoy something that you own?

_____
_____
_____
_____

> Your time is no more valuable than anyone else's. It is only valuable to you. You have the same amount of time in a day as everyone else does, so it is clearly how you use it and how you leverage every moment that counts.

CHAPTER 14
If Only I Had More Time

How could you use your time in a way that makes it an asset and something you truly cherish versus something that plagues you? Answer these questions and see how you can shift your thinking and ways of doing things to help you do a time inventory assessment and better leverage your time as one of your greatest assets.

How do you control how your time is spent? Are you doing anything that is eating away at your time on a regular basis that you wish you did not have to do?

_____
_____
_____
_____

What is taking time away from what you really want to be doing?

_____
_____
_____

What are you a slave to that distracts you from what you want to be spending your time doing?

_____
_____
_____
_____

Where do you believe your time is best spent?

What do you consider to be time wasters? Are some of these enjoyable? Why do you feel they are time wasters?

Of those time wasters that are not enjoyable, what can you do to avoid them? Is there someone else who can do them? Is there another way you can approach the situation to recapture some of your time?

How do you protect your time? Are you taking the initiative to offer options for your schedule, or are you allowing yourself to be at the mercy of everyone else's time?

Who in your work does not value your time? Can you make a change to work with someone who respects your time?

_____
_____
_____
_____

If someone in your family or work does not value your time or takes it for granted, can this be directly addressed and new expectations set? Make notes below for reference.

_____
_____
_____
_____

> Your passion is what gets your juices flowing toward whatever you are setting out to do. It's also what stirs such an emotion in you that it can frustrate instead of invigorate you, especially when the right support is not there when you need it.

CHAPTER 15
If Only I Had More Support

In order to gain the support you feel is missing, you must take a look at where support is lacking or counterproductive to your ultimate plan.

Who in your life is not supportive or simply does not seem to "get" what you are trying to achieve? Before you decide to eliminate them from your life, especially if they are a key part of your life like a spouse or family member, answer the following questions.

Are you supporting what they do? Are you engaged in what they do? Are you expressing interest in what they are trying to do?

_____

_____

_____

_____

When is the last time you sat down and really shared what you are trying to accomplish and what they could do to help support you?

_____

_____

_____

_____

Is there a common factor that could come into play that could bring you together in a mutually beneficial way? If yes, make notes below. Consider any common factor, no matter how insignificant it may seem.

_____
_____
_____

Have you identified and expressed ways in which achieving your goals can complement them achieving their goals?

_____
_____

Have they always been negative or unsupportive, or has this occurred only in respect to one particular issue or incident? If one of the latter, what is the underlying reason, and can it be resolved?

_____
_____
_____

Take a look at each goal that is getting nowhere or not progressing as effectively as you would like. Answer these questions to identify how you can rally more support.

Does your goal require input from a variety of perspectives? Could an advisory council serve a purpose in achieving the goal? Who could be on your advisory council? Hint: Who shares values related to top goals?

_____
_____
_____

Can you segment the goal into manageable pieces so that those who support you can take ownership of its progress in small pieces or projects to help you move it forward?

_____
_____
_____
_____

List the type of support needed for each goal and who is directly affected by the goal. Can these individuals contribute in some way? Do they know other resources you could tap into for support?

_____
_____
_____
_____

"An uncomfortable mindset exists when we venture into anything new or foreign to us. The ability to look inside yourself and acknowledge those aspects that keep you from making progress toward your goals is the first step toward finally realizing that you have nothing to fear."

SECTION 4

Fearful Thinking – From Fear to Inspired Action!

Does an underlying fear exist within you that is keeping you from achieving or going after something you would love to happen in your life? Or could it be that you can't quite understand why you are not able to make strides in what you are trying to achieve, as if something is holding you back or keeping you from what you truly desire?

The ability to look inside yourself and acknowledge those aspects that keep you from making progress toward your goals is the first step toward finally realizing your ultimate life. One of the first steps to overcoming fears is being able to see them, know how they exist in you, and then confront them.

This section is going to help you understand the fears that you are allowing to limit your progress. Seeing yourself and how you think in a new light will help you release your fears once and for all. You will begin to approach things in a different way. You will better understand what motivates you and what holds you back.

This kind of wisdom can only mean one thing – utter and total freedom and empowerment. Now that is exciting, isn't it?

"Success can only become tangible once you define what it means to you and only you. The reality is that we have small successes every day, and if leveraged properly, they add up to our ultimate success, created and determined from the inside out."

CHAPTER 16
Fear of Success

Let's take a look at your current perception of success to see if we can help you shift it in a more positive, effective direction. Answer these questions to gain insight about your views on success.

What are symbols of success for you? Are they material things or more intrinsic things? Who may have formed these ideas in your head?

_____

_____

_____

_____

What is your definition of success? Write down words that describe your idea of success and be as specific as you can.

_____

_____

_____

_____

Whom do you view as successful in a positive way and you would like to emulate? Why?

_____

_____

_____

Whom do you view as successful whom you would not want to emulate. Why? Has this affected decisions you have made or approaches you have taken that could be holding you back out of fear of being the same?

_____
_____
_____
_____

Has a major life occurrence shifted or evolved your idea of success and what is most important to achieve? If so, make notes below.

_____
_____
_____
_____

Now let's take a look at how your values have played into your idea of success. Pull out your Values Mind Map and compare it to your answers in this chapter. When it comes right down to what makes you feel fulfilled, what values come into play, and how does this translate to how you define success for yourself?

Write down below what your values are telling you that success means for you.

_____
_____
_____
_____

MM&I MOMENT OF INSPIRATION

*"If you can imagine it, it can be real.
If you have conceived the possibility,
it can be your probability."*

- Sherré DeMao -

"Failure is an illusion. Everything you do produces a result. Some results were what you desired, and some did not turn out exactly as you had hoped. This doesn't mean you failed. It means you have been enlightened."

CHAPTER 17
Fear of Failure

Answering the "why" and "why not" questions forces you to look at reality – your reality – versus imagined factors. What it also does is help you take an honest look at each reason you cite and objectively refute or validate. You will be putting the reasons to move forward with an idea and the reasons that are holding you back side by side. Then you move on to the "why not me" and "why not now" questions. These often help you put things into even clearer perspective as you explore your answers.

Next to all the reasons "not," note what is in your control, what could be in your control, and what is outside of your control. Focus on those things that are within your control. Then stop procrastinating and put these things into action. Pretty soon, you too will have a much different view of failure. I guarantee it.

Avoiding Failure

Make a list of goal-related activities that you procrastinate about, keeping you from taking the next step toward your goal.

_____

_____

WHY? *Why should I still consider going for it?*

_____

_____

WHY NOT? *What is holding me back, or what am I perceiving as an obstacle?*

_____

_____

WHY NOT ME? *What about me specifically could be a reason that I would not succeed?*

_____

_____

WHY ME? *What about me are reasons why I could succeed?*

_____

_____

WHY NOW? *Why is now a good time?*

_____

_____

WHY NOT NOW? *What could make this not be a good time and why?*

_____

_____

Perceived Failure

Make a list of things you have attempted to do that did not work out as planned. Then ask yourself these questions.

_____

_____

WHY? *Why should I consider going for it again? Would I still really like to achieve it?*

_____

_____

WHY NOT? *What is holding me back? Or what could still pose an obstacle?*

_____

_____

WHY ME? *What about me have I learned that could make it achievable now?*

_____

_____

WHY NOT ME? *What about me specifically could be a reason that I would still not succeed?*

_____

_____

WHY NOW? *Why is now a good time?*

_____

_____

WHY NOT NOW? *What could make this not be a good time and why?*

_____

_____

> The mindset that nobody does it better than you can cripple you when it is applied to everything you do or touch. When we attempt to control everything and everyone to the point of inaction, then we are not fully aware that we are the ones holding everything back.

CHAPTER 18
Fear of Losing Control

Take a look at one or more of your goals that you have been trying to accomplish without making much progress at the moment. Answer these questions.

What are things that you are controlling, and hence, nothing is getting done?

_____
_____
_____
_____

Why, since you are controlling it, has no progress been made?

_____
_____
_____
_____

Are there any elements out of your control that are affecting your ability to control? If so, what are they?

_____
_____
_____
_____

Is anything in your control that you wish someone else could take control of? Do you feel like you are the only one that can do it properly? Why do you feel this way, and is it real or imagined? Be honest. If it would be a relief to hand it off, then do it!

_____
_____
_____
_____

What areas are you micromanaging, but don't want to micromanage? Why do you feel this way? What could be the next step toward taking charge to no longer having to micromanage it?

_____
_____
_____
_____

Is there anything that you feel only you can do that could be documented or written down into a system or procedure that then could be handled by others? Really think about this one because this is where you can maintain control without having to be in control of it.

_____
_____
_____
_____

In what areas do you not want to lose control and why? Are these valid reasons? Explain why they are valid reasons for not losing control.

What are some of the little incidental things that you find yourself doing out of sheer habit, that are really not about control at all, but about getting it done? Are these things draining you from other more important things? Are there others that could easily take these things off your plate and free you to do what you really want to be doing?

> Without making attempts to go further, we may never stumble across those opportunities that open a whole new world to us. Some of our greatest 'aha' moments happen while we are striving toward something else.

CHAPTER 19
Fear of Taking Risks

After answering these questions, look at all of your answers as a whole. Chances are, you will begin to see some correlations between your successes. In addition, you may see that you did not explore all possibilities in some of your attempts that did not work out as planned. Answer these questions to begin to explore the possibilities.

Think back to some of the biggest risks that you have taken and succeeded. What were the elements that contributed to the success? How did you overcome any obstacles?

_____

_____

_____

Consider small risks that you have taken that have paid off. Why were they small risks comparatively speaking? What made them less risky and why?

_____

_____

_____

What, if you had to do it all over again, would you have done sooner, but the risk factor kept you from taking the plunge? Looking back, why do you now wish you would not have hesitated? If you had not hesitated, what new result do you believe you may have realized?

_____

_____

_____

What risks have you taken that did not turn out as you had hoped or work out as planned? What contributed to these results? What could you have tried or done differently? As a result of this risk not paying off, what have you determined? Are you actually settling for less? Are there resources you did not tap or consider that could have helped you overcome any obstacles?

___

What are some risks that you would like to take, but are hesitant to take? Why are you hesitant? What is the worst-case scenario, and what is the best-case scenario? What resources beyond your own means could you tap to achieve this?

___

What are you doing personally to challenge yourself? If nothing, what would you like to discover or learn that interests you? What would it take to explore this interest? What are your reasons for not pursuing it?

___

MM&I MOMENT OF INSPIRATION

*"It takes elevated thinking
to realize next-level results."*

- Sherré DeMao -

> Look around at everyone in a crowd at any given moment, and there is something extraordinary about the fact that no two people look alike. Even identical twins have unique aspects that make each one unlike the other. The reality is that each of us is unique, and there is nothing ordinary about that.

CHAPTER 20
Fear of Being Ordinary

Do you fully understand how special you are? Do you fully embrace that there is a YOU-niqueness about you that cannot be duplicated, just merely emulated?

Yet many of us will go to great lengths to either disappear in the abyss of others, believing we are nothing special, OR stand out at all costs in order to NOT be viewed as ordinary.

I have a magnet on my refrigerator that claims, "The only normal people are people you don't know that well." I love that magnet because it speaks the truth. Get to know anyone, and you will find something special, unique, quirky, whatever it may be. It makes them, well, them. Just like the nuances of you make you, well, you.

When you have a fear of being ordinary, the response is two extremes.

The first extreme is believing that you are just ordinary, and this fear that you are really nothing special keeps you bound in a web of inaction, disinterest, and disbelief that you deserve anything special at all.

The second extreme is a defiance of being ordinary to the point of taking action and making decisions to prove how opposite of ordinary you can be. It can get to the point of being destructive and disruptive in ways that hurt more than help you.

Either way, you can be so caught up in either of the extremes that you are not allowing yourself to know the absolute extraordinariness that exists within you just waiting to blossom, nor are you allowing yourself to express your true self and naturally be.

Nothing Special

When you fear that you are only ordinary and nothing special, and it is accepted as a fact in your mind, then you succumb to this belief and believe this is the lot you have been given. You view everyone around you as better and more special. Why has this occurred? What has caused you to accept this way of thinking about yourself?

As a child growing up, did someone instill this thinking into you? If so, who, and what was it they made you believe?

_____

_____

If no one has influenced you directly, what else has impacted this belief? Write whatever comes to mind.

_____
_____
_____

Why do you believe you are just ordinary and nothing special?

_____
_____
_____

What is something that you can do that someone else you know cannot do? Name anything at all, no matter how insignificant you believe it to be.

_____
_____
_____
_____

Determined NOT to be ordinary

Those who are determined NOT to be ordinary tend to fall into the daredevil, defiant, and high-risk-taker categories. Being unique is emphasized in actions, appearance, and attitude. Standing out is important and quite evident as a part of how they behave. Is this you? Are you trying too hard at NOT being ordinary?

Whether in the past or currently, have you done something intentionally to your appearance to stand out or be different? If yes, note what has been done or is being done currently to stand out or be different.

_____
_____
_____
_____

Are you an extreme risk taker? Do you love a good challenge, enjoy pushing yourself to the edge of even safety or caution? If so, give some examples below.

_____
_____
_____
_____

Are you continuously out to prove something to others or someone in particular? If so, what and who is so important that you feel you must prove this about yourself? Why?

_____
_____
_____
_____

Are you driven to excel and to win? Do you believe that winning is a measure of your uniqueness and proof of not being ordinary? List some examples below.

_____
_____
_____
_____

Is there anything you have done that wasn't really comfortable or true to whom you feel you are, but you did it anyway just to prove you are not ordinary? If so, list here and note why you felt you needed to do it at that time.

_____
_____
_____
_____

> "There is a difference between being busy and being actively engaged in your efforts to achieve. If you are doing things that are keeping you busy yet not moving you forward, it is time to let go of them. Now."

CHAPTER 21
Fear of Letting Go

With responsibility comes awareness more than anything else. That awareness begins with recognizing that what you desire is entirely reliant on your ability to decipher what is the best possible use of your time, talent, and energy.

Are there any projects or initiatives you are currently working on that have not been launched for the rest of the world to see? If yes, then list them below and then answer the questions.

_____

_____

_____

_____

Are you finding that you are holding something up because of a desire to make it better, higher quality, or something else? What are these reasons, and are they really going to make or break its success for a launch? Could it be launched and continually improved?

_____

_____

_____

_____

When do you expect to officially introduce the initiative? Have you set an introduction or launch date? If not, why not?

_____
_____
_____

If you move forward with introducing this as it currently is, what would be the worst that could happen? Is this scenario a true possibility or simply an excuse to keep holding it back?

_____
_____
_____
_____

What made you start the initiative in the first place? Is this still valid and appropriate for where your life and desires are currently?

_____
_____
_____

Are there other initiatives or projects you have on the back burner that could be more important, but you believe this one must be finished first? If it is no longer as important, could it be that it is in this quagmire because your passion is no longer in it? List these other initiatives you could be doing here. Also, note why your passion has waned on what you believe you must get done first, as well as why you believe it must get done first.

_____
_____
_____

What would happen if you abandoned this project or initiative? Note what you think could happen. Could abandoning it altogether actually free you to focus on more relevant work? How?

_____
_____
_____
_____

If it is still deemed of value and merit, could other resources be pulled in to help bring it to completion? If so, list some of what you would need below.

_____
_____
_____
_____

Are there any commitments that you have made either personally or professionally that you find are no longer enjoyable, satisfying, or that you simply dread yet believe that you must fulfill because of your strong sense of obligation and doing as promised? If yes, list them below and then answer the questions.

_____
_____
_____

Why did you make the commitment in the first place? Was it truly centered from your desire or someone else's?

_____
_____
_____
_____

Is this a commitment that holds great significance in your life, but has changed unexpectedly? How has it changed, and what this change caused as a result?

_____
_____
_____
_____

Are any of your other values being sacrificed as a result of this obligation being fulfilled? What are they?

_____
_____
_____
_____

Why has this become an unsatisfying or unfulfilling commitment?

_____
_____
_____
_____

Is there a way to refocus this commitment to better align it with what you can be passionate about or motivated to fulfill? Restate it now and see if this makes a difference. If you cannot restate it, then it may be time to let it go.

_____
_____
_____
_____

Is there someone else who could take over this commitment and therefore fulfill the promise without you having to be ultimately responsible? If yes, list some potential people you know or would like to know.

_____
_____
_____
_____

> Because it makes so much sense, because it is logical and comfortable, and most important of all, because it is doable, you too can put synergy in motion. Synergy is a natural part of you once you embrace the three aspects of you and drive everything you do from within.

SECTION 5

Synergy in Motion

Now that you understand that Work/Life Balance is externally focused, you can shift with total confidence to the beautiful joy of synergizing you and all you were meant to become.

Now that you have gained insight to what may be limiting you through wishful or fearful thinking, it is time to leave these limiting factors and beliefs behind once and for all. It is time to put the synergy within you into motion toward the ultimate life you deserve to live and love.

This section will help you totally shift to synergy as your way of being to truly experiencing a synergized world, an energized you, and living your ultimate life.

> If you know your purpose and are on a true mission to fulfill that purpose, then what results is an explosion of opportunities, serendipities, and an unwavering focus to see it through in each moment of the rest of your life.

CHAPTER 22
The Power of Purpose

I believe without doubt that each of us was put on this earth for a purpose, a profound purpose. You are here for a reason; one that no one else can fulfill in quite the same way. We are all connected to bring our purpose to the forefront, helping one another realize one another's ultimate purpose. How powerful is this? It is life-changing powerful.

Your values say a lot about who you are and what is most important to you. Take a look at those values you starred on your Values Mind Map. Write these values here. NOTE: Only the values you starred and deemed most important should go here.

_____

_____

_____

_____

Your ultimate benefits of your values and your ultimate outcomes of your goals also say a great deal about what is important to you. Write the ultimate benefits and ultimate outcomes you stated.

Ultimate Benefits	**Ultimate Outcomes**

Answer these questions to help you define even further your personal purpose and mission … your reason for being.

For you personally, what do you enjoy doing or how do you enjoy being more than anything else in the world?

_____
_____
_____
_____

When do you feel you are making a real difference? What are you doing? How does this impact others and make you feel as a result?

_____
_____
_____
_____

What is the one thing that makes you passionate and excited over anything else? How can you use this in creating your ultimate purpose?

_____
_____
_____
_____

If you own a business, or in your work, what is your company ultimately trying to do for the markets you serve? Is this personally gratifying for you? If so, how?

_____
_____
_____
_____

What is the difference your business or the work you do is trying to make for your customer, industry, or marketplace that no other company is currently doing as well or at all? Is this exciting to you? Is this meaningful to you?

_____
_____
_____
_____

What are you trying to prove can be done that has not been done in quite the same way before in your work or in areas that you give back?

_____
_____
_____
_____

What legacy would you like to leave behind as a result of your purpose? How would you like to be remembered? Place descriptive words below.

_____
_____
_____

Based on the answers to the questions in this section, are there any additional values you need to add to your Values Mind Map? If so, add these values to your map and use the answers in this section to cite your reasons and complete the Values Mind Map diagram. Note these values below as a reference before beginning to add to your Mind Map.

_____
_____
_____
_____

Creating Your Purpose Statement

Now look at your Values Mind Map again. Do any of these newly added values deserve a star/asterick or a check mark? How does the order of your values change as a result of these additions? Make these changes as inspired, and then we will proceed.

EXAMPLE: Below is my own example in order for you to better understand how to begin to process your values into your purpose mission statement.

Values = ★ At Core of YOU
1. New thinking/innovation/creativity
2. Positivity/optimism
3. Seeing possibilities/opportunities
4. Nurturing growth/next level

Values = ✔ Important to YOU
A. Excellence/realizing great value
B. Embracing uniqueness
C. Life-long learning
D. Open-mindedness/flexibility/adaptability
E. Independence/self-reliance

FINAL RESULTING PURPOSE MISSION STATEMENT
My purpose is to inspire new thinking to empower positive outcomes by seeing what others see yet think what no one else has thought. I accomplish this by helping companies and individuals learn to: realize their next level of growth and accomplishment; embrace their next idea and YOU-niqueness; and achieve their greatest value and bliss.

Now that you have seen an example, take another look at your Values Mind Map and all the values you have starred and checked. List them again below for reference in their order of priority based on your notations from your Mind Map.

Values with ★ = At Core of YOU   **Values with ✔ = Important to YOU**

_____   _____
_____   _____
_____   _____
_____   _____
_____   _____
_____   _____
_____   _____
_____   _____

PURPOSE MISSION STATEMENT: In the section below, there are several series of fill-ins for you to complete a variety of mission statements based on your prioritized values. Complete and adapt until you have crafted one that feels like it represents everything you believe you can be for others.

My purpose is to _____ through

_____
_____
_____

I accomplish this by _____

_____
_____
_____

My purpose is to _____ through

_____
_____
_____

I accomplish this by _____

_____
_____
_____

My purpose is to _____ *through*

_____
_____
_____

I accomplish this by _____

_____
_____
_____

My purpose is to _____ *through*

_____
_____
_____

I accomplish this by _____

_____
_____
_____

My purpose is to _____ *through*

_____
_____
_____

I accomplish this by _____
_____
_____
_____

***My purpose** is to* _____ *through*
_____
_____
_____

I accomplish this by _____
_____
_____
_____

***My purpose** is to* _____ *through*
_____
_____
_____

***My purpose** is to* _____ *through*
_____
_____
_____

***My purpose** is to* _____ *through*
_____
_____
_____

I accomplish this as a result of my ability to _____
_____
_____
_____

***My purpose** is to* _____ *through*
_____
_____
_____

I accomplish this as a result of my ability to _____
_____
_____
_____

MM&I MOMENT OF INSPIRATION

"When your vision and purpose are clear, your options and choices are clearer."

- Sherré DeMao -

> Hope is the one thing that can inspire alternatives when it seems that there is nothing you can do in a particular situation. You believe there has to be an option; therefore, you seek to understand, learn, or find the options.

CHAPTER 23
The Power of HOPE

Hoping is looking forward into the future. One of my favorite quotes by Helen Keller reads, "Hope sees the invisible, feels the intangible, and achieves the impossible." This is such a powerful statement and one that demonstrates how being hopeful is so much more empowering than being wishful.

Hope stems from and is supported by your values, reinforced by them to continually seek additional options and answers. Hope is action-oriented because it is trying to see beyond the current circumstance or events happening to you or around you. Hope reaches deeper into who you are to manifest who you ultimately know you can be.

Having hope means you possess a faith in yourself to achieve or prevail in whatever you are faced with or must overcome. You truly believe in the best possible outcome and are focused on looking forward into not only its possibility, but also how to affect its probability.

Bring hope into your being. Make hope your way of being. Move forward with your heart, optimism, passion, and effort guiding and leading you every step of the way. Consider these aspects of hope to help make your hopeful thinking stronger and to shift from any of the wishful thinking you processed in Section V.

H = Heart: Hope stems from your heart, the very center of how you feel, what you believe, and what inspires your faith in yourself. When you have your heart into whatever you are doing, it is not only easier to do, but also satisfying and gratifying. Knowing your values and what you hold to be true to you is the first step in shifting from wishful thinking to hope. Add to this a list of those who share the same values, and you have a built-in network of resources to help you.

Write your top values below and who shares these specific values as a reminder of whom you may be able to turn to for seeing options and positive ways you can move forward.

_____

_____

_____

O = Optimism: Too often, in wishful thinking, you are focused on what you don't want to occur more than what you truly want to occur. The negative is overriding the positive in making you wish for something different or better. You see obstacles and have doubts that keep you complacent in a wishful mode. In some cases, you may even proclaim a wish, but it is merely an excuse to keep you from taking the necessary action. Your pessimism paralyzes you into a feeling of hopelessness because of what you fear added to the wishful mindset. To move forward, you must face your fears using your heart network. That heart network includes those who share your values. With hope, you truly believe in the possibilities. Your optimism enables you to see options to help you through any given situation and continually reinforces and empowers you.

For anything that you are currently doubting or frustrated by, note someone who shares your values or whom you know to be an optimistic and positive influence, and note what they might say you could do. Or better yet, ask them what they would do.

_____

_____

_____

_____

_____

P = Passion: When your heart combines with optimism, your passion is given wings to soar toward the very best outcome you seek. Passion is the very aura of your values rolled into who you are and why you are driven to do what you do. Passion gives you energy to prevail, persevere, and participate in making whatever it is you hope will occur into what does occur.

What are you most passionate about based on your purpose that you can focus upon right now, and what action can you take?

_____

_____

_____

_____

_____

E = Effort: Even if you can see the invisible and feel the intangible, without effort on your part, you will never make what seems to be impossible happen. It really is that simple. Your effort reinforces to yourself that what you hope and desire is truly important to you and for you to manifest.

Note below up to ten actions you can take putting your heart, optimism, and passion into motion to make the effort real and specific.

1.
2.
3.
4.
5.
6.
7.
8.
9.
10.

"Goals viewed together become a stronger possibility. Goals planned together become a distinct probability. Understanding the connections that exist between what you want to achieve short term and long term can be the tipping point to realizing everything you desire faster than originally anticipated."

CHAPTER 24
Short-Term & Long-Term Insights

Gaining a holistic view of your goals that powerfully connects them within your mind will help you make new connections you would have otherwise never made.

Now it's time for you to examine your goals using this new mindset. Take a look at your reasons for your goals, your expected outcomes, who is impacted, and what people or resources are needed. You will find yourself more readily making associations between one goal and another.

You will start to see goals that impact the same people or goals that may require the support of the same type of people. You will look at those goals that appear to be in conflict in a new way. Before you know it, they are no longer in conflict as you find solutions and options you never considered before. You will start to look at your long-term and short-term goals on both sides and begin to consider how they can work together to achieve the long term faster and the short term easier. You will no longer have a career or business plan separate from your personal life, but a *life plan* that gets down to the business of helping you realize what you ultimately want to realize in your lifetime.

And with this realization, you have made the first critical step toward truly synergizing your world into *your* ultimate reality. You will be better able to assess what you need, what your options are, and what your next steps can be. This is also a good time to remind you of the three promises in Section II: finding a way or making a way by helping others find a way or make a way; not feeling guilty about making life easier for yourself; and being open to all possible options, resources, and support.

1. **First, go through your Goals Mind Map and mark each goal as either a short-term (ST) or long-term (LT) goal.** Short term will be defined as to be achieved within one to three years, and long term will be defined as longer than three years.

2. **Second, get out your Values Mind Map.**

3. **Get out some highlighters in multiple colors.** Highlight similar reasons for your goals in one color. Highlight similar resources or people needed in other colors of highlighter. Highlight people who are affected by your goals and the same people who share any specific values in the same color. Make notes of your observations below.

_____

_____

_____

_____

4. **Using the matrix below, place your short-term goals alongside your long-term goals.** See if you can make any connections based on what you have highlighted. Look at the ME, MYSELF, and INC. goals as a whole as you view them below along with what you have highlighted.

ME – Short Term Goals	ME – Long Term Goals
1.	1.
2.	2.
3.	3.
4.	4.

MYSELF – Short Term Goals	MYSELF – Long Term Goals
1.	1.
2.	2.
3.	3.
4.	4.

INC. – Short Term Goals	INC. – Long Term Goals
1.	1.
2.	2.
3.	3.
4.	4.

Study the similarities to see how they could possibly work together.

_____
_____
_____

1. How can you leverage the same resources to achieve all that you are setting out to do?

_____
_____
_____

2. How can you leverage those who share your values who could provide support or perspective toward certain goals?

_____
_____
_____

3. Who could help you look at these goals in unison and offer some creative solutions based on the resources needed?

_____
_____
_____
_____

> "The reality is that you can do a lot more than you realize. It starts with shifting from focusing on what you can't do or don't have control over to what you can do, no matter how small of an action it may be."

CHAPTER 25
Your Action Plan – The Power of CAN DO

The real shift from *can't* to *can* occurs when you begin to make it a habit to have a can-do attitude no matter what gets thrown at you. A while ago, I gave additional meaning to having a can-do attitude to help inspire me, and have since inspired thousands. I created an acronym to give even more powerful meaning to CAN DO.

CAN DO = Conscientious Action Nurtures Desired Outcome.

Consider what this could mean for you to help you get back on track toward realizing your dreams. It is dream doing through synergy in motion!

C = Conscientious. Being conscientious about what you are striving to do means you are being intentional about it in everything that you do. It is not something you are going to get around to doing. It is something you believe is so important and will bring such value to you and others that it is worth being top of mind and at the forefront of your priorities in making it happen. You think about it every day and what can be done to take you a step closer to where you want to be every day.

As you read this description, what came to mind specifically for you?

_____

_____

_____

_____

A = Action. You can think all you want, but without "conscientious *action*" it will just remain in the "want to do" category instead of the "getting to do" realm. Once you bring what you want into a conscientious state of being, you then also need to attach that awareness and intent with real action. Don't let the dream itself overwhelm or intimidate you. Instead, allow it to inspire you to identify small actions you can take each and every day. Is it getting more information? Is it learning something? Is it connecting with someone? Breaking down the big dream into small steps toward achieving it will make it seem not only more real and also more achievable.

As you read this description, what came to mind specifically for you?

_____
_____
_____
_____

N = Nurtures. By taking conscientious action every day, you are nurturing your dream by making progress of some kind every day. It also means that you are nurturing and taking care of yourself by giving yourself permission to put some of your energy every day toward what you desire most in your life or work to happen. Nurturing is caring: caring about you, your future, and others who may benefit from this dream and desire becoming reality.

As you read this description, what came to mind specifically for you?

_____
_____
_____
_____

D = Desired. Another reason we can feel so frustrated in life is because we are spending most of our time doing what we really don't want to be doing. Why is this? When you take conscientious action nurturing what you truly desire, you also find that you are truly enjoying the journey in getting there. You are feeling more satisfied even before you realize the full outcome because you are doing what you really want to be doing, and it feels more fulfilling. Take an honest look at what you truly desire as it relates to your goal, and it will make it that much easier to identify the actions you need to take on an ongoing basis to get you where you want to go.

As you read this description, what came to mind specifically for you?

_____

_____

_____

_____

O = Outcome: Once you achieve this goal, realize this dream or desire you have, what will be the outcome? Go back and look at your Goals Mind Map and review what you have put as your ultimate outcomes. Really try to articulate this as it is that important to understand. What will it ultimately mean to you and for others in your life? If you don't fully know the answer to this, then this could also be a part of your problem. Being able to envision what your life will be like after you achieve what you want to achieve helps make it more real and more tangible. It also helps you better identify opportunities and make better decisions because you understand what it will mean for you in the end.

As you read this description, what came to mind specifically for you?

_____

_____

_____

_____

Having a CAN-DO attitude means that you believe in what you are doing and the impact it will have in your life and for others as well. You are unstoppable because you believe in options, possibilities, opportunities, and your own ability to make things happen.

Some days, your action may just be taking a few meditative moments to re-engage your vision, so you can refocus your action to allow you to process and best choose your next best steps. Other days, you will have a variety of actions moving your dream forward. The most important thing is to keep what you want most to happen in your life top of mind and within your heart.

Start each day focused on what you CAN DO, and before you know it, you will be doing and enjoying all that you hoped you could be doing.

Based on your Goals Mind Map, list below your top two short-term and long-term goals for each aspect of you. We will dive deeper with each of these on the next pages.

ME Aspect

Short Term	Long Term
1.	1.
2.	2.

MYSELF Aspect

Short Term	Long Term
1.	1.
2.	2.

INC. Aspect

Short Term	Long Term
1.	1.
2.	2.

Your Action Plan: Focusing on your top two short-term (ST) and long-term (LT) goals in each area of ME, MYSELF, and INC., begin to compose your action plan below.

ME ST Goal #1:			CAN-DO ACTION STEPS
OPTIONS	RESOURCES	PEOPLE	1.
			2.
			3.
			4.
			5.
			6.
			7.

ME LT Goal #1:			CAN-DO ACTION STEPS
OPTIONS	RESOURCES	PEOPLE	1.
			2.
			3.
			4.
			5.
			6.
			7.

_____

_____

_____

_____

ME ST Goal #2::			CAN-DO ACTION STEPS
OPTIONS	RESOURCES	PEOPLE	1.
			2.
			3.
			4.
			5.
			6.
			7.

ME LT Goal #2:			CAN-DO ACTION STEPS
OPTIONS	RESOURCES	PEOPLE	1.
			2.
			3.
			4.
			5.
			6.
			7.

_____

_____

_____

_____

_____

_____

_____

MYSELF ST Goal #1::			CAN-DO ACTION STEPS
OPTIONS	RESOURCES	PEOPLE	1.
			2.
			3.
			4.
			5.
			6.
			7.

MYSELF LT Goal #1:			CAN-DO ACTION STEPS
OPTIONS	RESOURCES	PEOPLE	1.
			2.
			3.
			4.
			5.
			6.
			7.

_____
_____
_____
_____
_____
_____
_____

MYSELF ST Goal #2:			CAN-DO ACTION STEPS
OPTIONS	**RESOURCES**	**PEOPLE**	1.
			2.
			3.
			4.
			5.
			6.
			7.

MYSELF LT Goal #2:			CAN-DO ACTION STEPS
OPTIONS	**RESOURCES**	**PEOPLE**	1.
			2.
			3.
			4.
			5.
			6.
			7.

_____
_____
_____
_____
_____
_____
_____

INC. ST Goal #1:			CAN-DO ACTION STEPS
OPTIONS	RESOURCES	PEOPLE	1.
			2.
			3.
			4.
			5.
			6.
			7.

INC. LT Goal #1:			CAN-DO ACTION STEPS
OPTIONS	RESOURCES	PEOPLE	1.
			2.
			3.
			4.
			5.
			6.
			7.

_____

_____

_____

_____

_____

_____

_____

INC. ST Goal #2:			CAN-DO ACTION STEPS
OPTIONS	**RESOURCES**	**PEOPLE**	1.
			2.
			3.
			4.
			5.
			6.
			7.

INC. LT Goal #2:			CAN-DO ACTION STEPS
OPTIONS	**RESOURCES**	**PEOPLE**	1.
			2.
			3.
			4.
			5.
			6.
			7.

_____
_____
_____
_____
_____
_____
_____

MM&I MOMENT OF INSPIRATION

"Your willpower is your greatest asset to achieving once you believe that you will and you give yourself the power."

- Sherré DeMao -

ABOUT THE AUTHOR

Sherré DeMao is founder, CEO, and Strategy Maestro of BizGrowth Inc, an award-winning firm specializing in next-level, next-idea solutions for entrepreneurs with a focus on building sustainable value while making a significant difference. She is an expert in helping entrepreneurs prosper in life and in business, and has dedicated her 30-year career to this purpose. Her business acumen, advocacy, and innovative approach to advising and working with entrepreneurs has resulted in national recognition including being honored with a Small Business Woman Champion Award (2006) by the Small Business Administration, named among North America's 50 Most Enterprising Women (2007), and an International Consultancy Award by *Corporate Vision Magazine* (2015). In 2018, Sherré was featured among *Huffington Post's* Thrive Global "Women of the C-Suite." A nationally acclaimed author, speaker, and impassioned researcher, she is currently conducting a groundbreaking study linking a company's stock value to corporate culture. Her book, *Me, Myself & Inc.*, introduced an alternative Life Synergy approach for entrepreneurs versus Work/Life Balance, resulting in her being the subject matter expert for chapter 2, also called *Me, Myself & Inc.*, in the university text *Smart Start-up Business Management*.

Sherré DeMao's passion is inspiring new thinking to empower positive outcomes. Her thought leadership, through speaking and *Dream Wide Awake* blog and ezine, inspires people around the globe to embrace their own power in realizing their ultimate lives. As a Certified Growth Strategist to entrepreneurs, Sherré helps business owners and their team members realize true satisfaction and prosperity personally and professionally. She was inspired to develop this companion workbook to *Me, Myself & Inc.* in order to bring a tool that could help every person on this planet know their "why" and reason for being. Sherré believes that opportunities abound. It's just a matter of thinking beyond what you see, visioning beyond what you think, and embracing your unique talents and gifts.

Did you know Sherré is available for multiday
Dream Wide Awake retreats for your team or organization?
If you are interested in having a retreat, email **inspired@sherredemao.com**
for more information. You can also obtain *Dream Wide Awake* on audio
via Audible for a self-guided retreat with the printed workbook.

www.ingramcontent.com/pod-product-compliance
Lightning Source LLC
Chambersburg PA
CBHW050500110426
42742CB00018B/3320